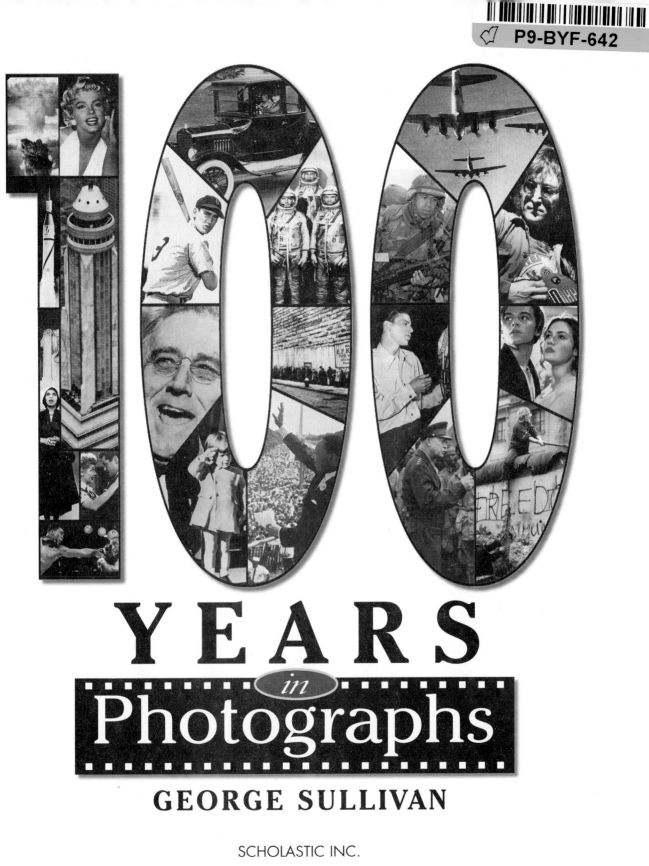

100

YEARS

in

Photographs

GEORGE SULLIVAN

SCHOLASTIC INC.

New York   Toronto   London   Auckland   Sydney   Mexico City   New Delhi   Hong Kong

ISBN 0-590-22858-7

Copyright © 1999 by George Sullivan.
All rights reserved. Published by Scholastic Inc.
SCHOLASTIC and logos are trademarks and/or registered trademarks
of Scholastic Inc.

12 11 10 9 8 7 6 5 4 3 2 1   9/9 0 1 2 3 4/0

Printed in the U.S.A.   40
First Scholastic printing, January 1999

Table of Contents

Acknowledgments

In selecting the photographs to be used in this book, the author is grateful for the opportunity to have delved into the collections available at the National Archives at College Park, Maryland; the Prints and Photographs Division of the Library of Congress; the National Museum of American History, Smithsonian Institution; as well as the collections at many other of the nation's foremost historical and cultural institutions. In using these sources, the author was guided by a good number of archivists, librarians, historians, and photo researchers to whom he is most grateful. Special thanks are due the following: Mary Ison and Maya Keech, Prints and Photographs Division, Library of Congress; Allan Hart, National Museum of American History, Smithsonian Institution; James T. Parker II, Archival Research International; Linda Zemer, Chicago Historical Society; E. Philip Scott, Lyndon Baines Johnson Library; Pauline Testerman, Harry S. Truman Library; Kathleen A. Struss, Dwight D. Eisenhower Library; Kenneth G. Hafeli and Nancy Mirshah, Gerald R. Ford Library; and Kristine Kaske, National Air and Space Museum, Smithsonian Institution.

Special thanks are also due to Bebe Overmiller, Photoduplication Service, Library of Congress; Gwen Pitman, NASA; Bettie Sprigg, Department of Defense; Mary Yearwood, Schomburg Center for Research in Black Culture; Jack A. Green, Naval Historical Center; Frankie A. Lewis, Department of the Treasury; Tracey Kimball, New Mexico Legislative Council Service; India Spartz, Alaska Historical Collections; Chester Cowen, Oklahoma Historical Society; Laurie Devine, Department of Library, Archives, and Public Records, State of Arizona; Kathleen Ka'iulani de Silva, Governor's Office, State of Hawaii; Sal Alberti and James Lowe, James Lowe Autographs; Lt. Christopher J. Madden, News Photo Division, Department of the Navy; Patricia D. Kelly, National Baseball Hall of Fame and Museum; Daile Kaplan, Swann Galleries; Kathy Wohlschlaeger, University of Pennsylvania; Ellen LiBretto, Ballantine Books; Bill Fitzgerald and Carolyn McMahon, Wide World/Associated Press; William Asadorian, the Long Island Collection, Queensboro Public Library; and John Filo, Ed Wakin, and Bill Welling.

The author is also very grateful to Tim Sullivan for carefully reading and editing the manuscript and captions, a task that improved the book and helped to prevent his dad from making some critical errors. Thanks, Tim.

Introduction

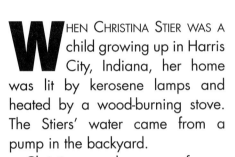

WHEN CHRISTINA STIER WAS A child growing up in Harris City, Indiana, her home was lit by kerosene lamps and heated by a wood-burning stove. The Stiers' water came from a pump in the backyard.

Christina was born on a farm near Harris City in 1902. Charles Lindbergh, the brave aviator who, in 1927, would make the first solo flight across the Atlantic, was born the same year. Theodore Roosevelt, whom everyone called Teddy, was president. Most Americans, like Christina, lived on farms.

When Christina was thirteen, the family moved "into town" — into nearby Greensburg. Life was better there, she remembers. In their Greensburg home, the Stiers had running water and the bathroom was indoors.

Electricity and the radio were still in the future. Automobiles were scarce; it was rare for Christina to see one. Family trips were made by horse and buggy.

Christina would have to wait almost half a century before watching television for the first time. She and her sisters often played games for entertainment — tag, hopscotch, or hide-and-seek. In the evenings, they enjoyed card games or checkers.

The work week was six days long in the early years of the century. People worked nine to ten hours a day. The average weekly wage was twelve dollars. Child labor was common.

The population of the United States was just over seventy-six million in 1900, less than a third of the population today. There were forty-five states in the United States.

The average life expectancy for whites was forty-seven years; for blacks, thirty-three years.

Christina married Gilbert Eder in 1927. The couple had three children, all girls.

When Christina turned ninety in 1992, her family held an open house at the Knights of St. John's Hall in Greensburg to celebrate the event. Hundreds of her friends and relatives turned out, including several of her many great-grandchildren. But the local newspaper, the *Greensburg Daily News*, didn't mention the event — evidence, perhaps, that living into one's nineties was no longer out of the ordinary.

In 1997, when this Introduction was written, Christina was looking forward to her ninety-sixth birthday. Her eyesight had failed, and she was a bit frail. "But she's still pretty spunky," said her youngest daughter, who was sixty-five.

According to Christina, "It's lots different now, much easier." During her lifetime, Christina saw the birth of electricity, radio, television, computers, home video, rockets, space travel — with men walking on the moon — penicillin, lasers, and vaccines for smallpox, polio, and measles.

It was an amazing century. The pages that follow are a photographic record of much of what happened.

THE 1900s
The New Century

OW DID PEOPLE DESCRIBE THE FIRST decade of the new century? Did they have a nickname for it, calling it the "ohs" or "double-ohs," the "aughts" or "naughts," or maybe simply the "hundreds"?

Old-timers say no, they didn't have any short, catchy term. The new decade was usually referred to as "the turn of the century" or something similar.

They could have called it "the decade of reform." Many Americans were discontented as the 1900s began, believing that the nation had grown at too reckless a pace during the last decades of the previous century.

The result was overcrowded cities, with slums and sweatshops, ruled by political bosses. Graft and corruption were commonplace. Big business was also guilty of alarming injustices.

The campaign for reform, for change, came to be known as the Progressive Movement. Two exceptional young men campaigned for Progressive goals — Robert La Follette, "Battlin' Bob," the governor of Wisconsin, who was elected to the U.S. Senate in 1905, and Theodore Roosevelt, who became president in 1901 after the assassination of William McKinley.

As president, the dynamic Roosevelt moved against big business and supported government regulation of the railroads. He got a pure food and drug act passed and called for the conservation of the nation's natural resources. Roosevelt helped to create the first national parks.

There were election reforms, too. The electoral process became more open, and voters were granted greater power in approving legislation and in removing corrupt public officials from office. The practice of choosing candidates through primary elections was established.

President Roosevelt caused an uproar in 1901 when he invited black educator Booker T. Washington to dine with him at the White House. During the late 1890s and early 1900s, the United States was a segregated society. In 1896, the Supreme Court had ruled that "separate but equal facilities" did not violate the Constitution. The ruling was a catastrophe for blacks, in that it gave government support to practicing discrimination.

Throughout the southern United States (where two-thirds of the nation's blacks lived in 1900), schools, trains, buses, and later lunch counters and drinking fountains and other arenas of daily life remained "separate" — but scarcely equal. White schools, for example, sometimes received ten times the funding of black schools.

Roosevelt's invitation to Booker T. Washington outraged many white Southerners. But blacks were heartened by the fact that Roosevelt appeared not to support racial segregation. Nevertheless, more than half a century would pass before important gains were made in the struggle against the separate-but-equal doctrine.

▼ On December 17, 1903, near Kitty Hawk, North Carolina, Wilbur and Orville Wright made history when they achieved powered, controlled flight in a heavier-than-air machine. They made four successful flights that day (one of which is pictured here, with Wilbur at the controls), the longest being 852 feet and lasting fifty-nine seconds.

(AP/Wide World)

◀ On McKinley's death, Vice President Theodore Roosevelt became president. A spirited man, full of energy, he hiked, camped, hunted, and played tennis and golf. Roosevelt achieved enormous popularity and won the 1904 election easily.

(Library of Congress)

The ten-story Home Insurance Building in Chicago, completed ▶ in 1885, is considered the first skyscraper. But the triangular-shaped Flatiron Building in New York City, right, which opened in 1902, soared twenty stories and became the model of countless skyscrapers to come.

(National Museum of American History)

◀ President William McKinley, in the first year of his second term, addresses a huge crowd at the Pan American Exposition in Buffalo, New York, on September 5, 1901. The next day, McKinley was shot by Leon Czolgosz. McKinley died on September 14, becoming the nation's third president to be assassinated. (Erie County Historical Society)

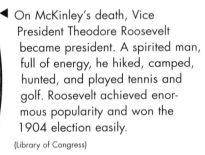

For more than half a century, Susan B. Anthony, pictured at right with her ▶
sister Mary, worked for women's rights, particularly the right to vote.
From 1892 to 1900, she headed the National American Woman
Suffrage Association. Earlier, she had worked with leading aboli-
tionists in the struggle to bring an end to slavery. The Nineteenth
Amendment, giving women the right to vote, became law in
1920, and in 1979 the Treasury Department issued a dollar
coin with Anthony's image on it. (Library of Congress)

◀ In 1903, Edwin S. Porter created *The Great Train Robbery*, the first film to
skillfully link one scene to another so as to create a plot that led to a cli-
max. Filmed in New Jersey, *The Great Train Robbery* was a huge success,
leading to other story films and to the opening of hundreds of nick-
elodeons, crude theaters that charged customers a nickel to watch such
presentations. This signaled the dawn of the movie industry. (Movie Star News)

Baseball's first modern World Series took place
in October 1903 when Boston in the American
League and Pittsburgh in the National League
met in a best-five-out-of-nine play-off, won by
Boston. In this scene, fans mill about the outfield
following a game at Huntington Avenue
Baseball Grounds in Boston.
(Baseball Hall of Fame and Library)

▲

In 1907, President Theodore Roosevelt sent sixteen American battleships with twelve thousand men aboard on a round-the-world voyage to demonstrate the military power of the United States. The ships came to be called the Great White Fleet.

(U.S. Naval Historical Center)

▲

Oklahoma joined the Union on November 16, 1907, as the forty-sixth state. Above, a parade on that date in Guthrie, Oklahoma, where the new state's constitution was drawn up, honors both the governor's Inauguration Day and Statehood Day. New Mexico and Arizona were admitted to the Union as the forty-seventh and forty-eighth states in 1912. (Oklahoma Historical Society)

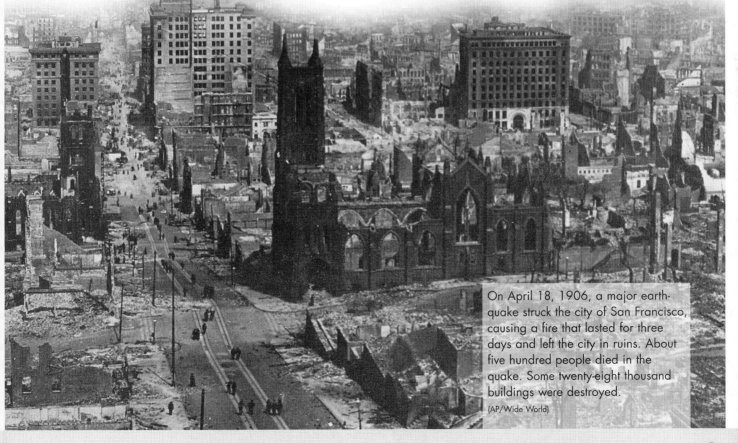

On April 18, 1906, a major earthquake struck the city of San Francisco, causing a fire that lasted for three days and left the city in ruins. About five hundred people died in the quake. Some twenty-eight thousand buildings were destroyed.

(AP/Wide World)

Henry Ford did not invent the automobile. But his Model T, introduced in 1909, was a perfected version of it. When Ford introduced assembly-line production, he was able to turn out Model Ts at the rate of one every twenty-four seconds. In 1914, Ford produced 248,000 Model Ts, about half of all the automobiles sold that year in the United States.
(AP/Wide World)

Commander Robert E. Peary claimed he was the first to reach the North Pole on foot, on April 6, 1909, even though five days earlier, Frederick Cook announced that he had already reached the pole. The National Geographic Society, the organization that sponsored Peary's venture, supports his claim, not Cook's. Today, Peary is generally credited as being the first to get to the pole.
(Library of Congress)

W. E. B. DuBois was an influential voice for black Americans during the 1900s. The first black to earn a Ph.D. from Harvard, DuBois taught, wrote, and lectured about what he called "the problem of the color line." In 1909, DuBois and his supporters founded the National Association for the Advancement of Colored People (NAACP).
(Schomburg Center for Research in Black Culture)

◄ Between 1901 and 1910, 8,798,838 immigrants entered the United States, more than at any other time in the nation's history. Most of the new arrivals came from eastern, central, and southern Europe. Here, a Jewish immigrant studies a Hebrew eye chart while undergoing a medical examination at Ellis Island in New York harbor. (Library of Congress)

◄ In the election of 1908, William Howard Taft, who promised to carry out the reforms begun by Theodore Roosevelt, won a decisive victory. Taft, who tipped the scales at around three hundred pounds, was the largest of the American presidents. (Library of Congress)

The appearance of Halley's Comet in 1909 generated widespread alarm. To many, the bright celestial body with its starlike center and long tail of cloudy light signaled that the end of the world was near. Halley's Comet was named for English astronomer Edmond Halley, who, in 1762, predicted its return.

(AP/Wide World)

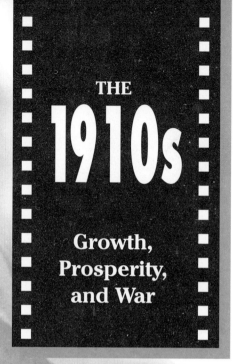

THE 1910s

Growth, Prosperity, and War

THE PROGRESSIVE MOVEMENT AND its agenda for reform, which thrived during the presidencies of Theodore Roosevelt and William Howard Taft, continued to flourish under Democrat Woodrow Wilson, who was elected president in 1912. Indeed, Wilson took Progressivism to new heights.

Under Wilson, Congress passed legislation that established the Federal Reserve System to regulate banking and the Federal Trade Commission to investigate unfair business practices on the part of large corporations. Congress also passed measures to curb the abuses of child labor and provide low-cost loans to farmers.

During the 1910s, several amendments to the Constitution were adopted, each reflecting an aspect of the Progressive Movement. One provided for an income tax, which was to become a major source of government revenue. Another amendment banned the manufacture and sale of alcoholic beverages.

For years, women had campaigned for voting rights. President Wilson, opposed to the idea at first, eventually came to favor it. Wilson supported and Congress approved the Nineteenth Amendment, which gave women the right to vote. It became law in 1920.

As the decade unfolded, concern in the United States with domestic reforms came to be overshadowed by a deepening crisis in international affairs. In August 1914, Austria-Hungary invaded the tiny republic of Serbia, its neighbor to the south. Within weeks, the major nations of Europe were at war with one another.

President Wilson issued a "proclamation of neutrality," calling for Americans to be "impartial in thought as well as action." The United States managed to remain uncommitted for three years, entering the war officially in April 1917.

The Great War, as it came to be called, was the most savage in history up until that time. It saw the first use of chemical weapons and the first bombings of civilians from the air.

By 1917, the bloody struggle, in which the German army advanced through Belgium deep into France, almost to Paris, was stalemated. The two million U.S. troops who were transported overseas helped tip the balance in favor of the British, French, and other Allied powers.

Peace arrived in November 1918. 112,000 Americans had lost their lives during World War I. (The Vietnam War, which lasted seven years, took the lives of 58,000 Americans.)

World War I was also known as the war to end all wars. It didn't happen, of course. Some twenty years later the international tensions that the war helped to produce would lead to another and even greater conflict.

A college teacher and later president of Princeton University, Democrat Woodrow Wilson was elected president of the United States in 1912 and won reelection in 1916. In 1919, Wilson helped to write the Treaty of Versailles and the Covenant of the League of Nations, both efforts to achieve lasting peace. (Library of Congress)

The *Titanic*, the largest and most luxurious ocean liner of its time, was believed to be the safest ship afloat. But at about 11:40 P.M. on April 14, 1912, on the vessel's first Atlantic crossing, from Southampton, England, to New York City, the *Titanic* struck an iceberg. Seawater flooded into the ship and two and a half hours later the ocean liner sank. A total of 1,517 people died in the disaster; there were 705 survivors.
(AP/Wide World)

On September 17, 1911, Calbraith Perry Rodgers took off from Sheepshead Bay, New York, in a rickety biplane built for him by the Wright brothers. He was to complete the first coast-to-coast flight across the United States. Two hours later, Rodgers landed in Middletown, New York, the first of sixty-eight short hops that the forty-nine-day journey required. (He also crash-landed nine times.)

◀ (National Air and Space Museum)

American women today have the same voting rights as men. But they did not gain such rights until the early 1900s, and they had to struggle for the better part of a century to get them. Their efforts involved marches and picketing. Above, suffragists, as those who supported voting rights for women were called, march in New York City in 1913. (Library of Congress)

On May 7, 1915, with World War I raging in Europe (but with the United States still on the sidelines), the British ocean liner *Lusitania* was torpedoed by a German submarine off the coast of Ireland, bringing death to 1,198 passengers and crew, 128 of them Americans. The great tragedy increased anti-German feeling in the United States. Below, the *Lusitania* begins its final voyage. (AP/Wide World)

American moviegoers of the 1910s adored the Little Tramp, a screen character created by comic genius Charlie Chaplin. At the age of twenty-seven, Chaplin signed a contract for a million dollars that called for him to deliver eight films in eighteen months. Chaplin was, along with Mary Pickford, one of the motion picture industry's first great stars. (Movie Star News)

Miss Jeannette Rankin

▲ After President Woodrow Wilson, who opposed women's suffrage at the time, was reelected in 1916, women began to picket around the clock outside the White House. Some chained themselves to the White House fence. These women were arrested at the White House following a suffrage demonstration in 1917.
(Library of Congress)

▲ A diligent campaigner for women's rights, Jeannette Rankin of Montana became the first woman elected to Congress when, in 1916, she won a seat in the House of Representatives. In 1917, Rankin voted against the United States entering World War I. In 1941, she cast the only vote against the entry of the United States into World War II.
(Library of Congress)

Construction of the forty-mile-long Panama Canal, a waterway linking the Atlantic and Pacific Oceans, began in 1906. The canal was opened to shipping in 1914, but gala opening ceremonies were canceled because of the war in Europe. (AP/Wide World)

▲

As the federal government expanded in size and influence during World War I, female clerical workers began to appear almost everywhere. These young women are the San Francisco Yeomanettes, who performed clerical duties for the Naval Reserve unit of the Twelfth Naval District. (National Archives)

▲

Known as "America's Sweetheart," Mary Pickford played young girls in *Poor Little Rich Girl* and *Rebecca of Sunnybrook Farm*, both released in 1917. She remained enormously popular through the 1920s. Pickford helped to found United Artists, with Douglas Fairbanks, and the Academy of Motion Picture Arts and Sciences. She earned an Academy Award for her performance in *Coquette*, released in 1929.

(Movie Star News)

During World War I, three million men were drafted, and a million more volunteered for military service. Of these four million, two million served overseas between 1917 and November 11, 1918, when the war ended. Here, soldiers undergo a final check before boarding a transport bound for France.

(AP/Wide World) ▶

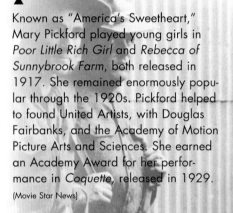

◀ A Salvation Army worker writes a letter home to the family of a soldier wounded during World War I. An estimated ten million died on the battlefields of Europe during the war. American losses were 112,000 dead and more than 200,000 wounded.
(National Archives)

On November 11, 1918, at 5 A.M., Germany signed an armistice treaty. Six hours later, at "the eleventh hour of the eleventh day of the eleventh month," the fighting ended in World War I. Below, soldiers at Camp Dix, New Jersey, celebrate their return to civilian life.
(National Archives)
▼

GOOD BYE
CAMP DIX

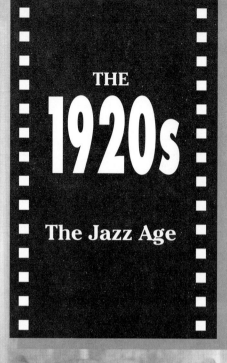

THE 1920s

The Jazz Age

THE 1920S WORE MANY LABELS, among them the Roaring Twenties, the Jazz Age, and the Era of Wonderful Nonsense. As this suggests, the 1920s was a time of frolic and foolishness, perhaps in reaction to World War I and its horrors.

Women, especially, adapted freer styles in appearance and behavior. They wore simpler and shorter dresses and cut their hair. They took up sports and drove automobiles.

There were "wild" parties where people danced the lively Charleston. "Confession" magazines appeared for the first time, as did the tabloids, heavily illustrated urban newspapers with sensational feature stories. "Ain't We Got Fun?" was a popular song of the day.

The 1920s was also a time of economic boom. With European nations weary and weak as a result of World War I, the United States emerged as the world's mightiest industrial power.

Automobiles were an important reason for this billing. In 1920, there were ten million cars on American highways. By 1929, there were twenty-nine million. Expanding automobile sales meant prosperity for the steel, glass, rubber, and oil industries.

New and improved consumer products were introduced, including vacuum cleaners, refrigerators (to replace home "iceboxes"), and a variety of electrical appliances. Commercial radio got started, and radio sets sold by the millions. New plastics and fibers spurred the chemical industry's growth.

But these were merely some of the more visible characteristics of American life during the 1920s. Prosperity did not touch everyone. The American farmer saw little reason to celebrate. Food prices plummeted, cutting farmers' incomes drastically. Four million Americans left their farms during the 1920s. There was no prosperity for miners, either; they earned seventy-five to eighty-five cents an hour.

Even more disturbing was the plight of American blacks. The great majority of all blacks still lived in the segregated South as the decade began, and they lived in rural locations, cut off from the opportunities presented by the nation's booming industries. Migrating to northern cities was no solution. Craft unions worked to deny membership to blacks. Only poor-paying service jobs were available.

The 1920s ended with a jolt. Republican Herbert Hoover became president on March 4, 1929. On October 29, the stock market, which had zoomed ever upward during the decade, nosedived. A long and severe economic depression quickly followed. "Ain't We Got Fun?" was replaced by "Brother, Can You Spare a Dime?"

Radio stations in all parts of the United States began broadcasting during the 1920s. Here, a young boy learns to draw by listening to lessons broadcast on station WOR. The trumpetlike loudspeaker was typical of early radio receivers. (Library of Congress)

In the presidential election of 1920, the first in which women could vote, Republican Warren G. Harding won by a comfortable margin. Harding delegated much of his power to members of his cabinet, party leaders, and members of Congress. Left, Harding poses with his pet dog, Laddie.

(Library of Congress)

Prohibition, the banning of the manufacture and sale of alcoholic ▶ beverages, became a reality after Congress approved the Eighteenth Amendment to the Constitution and adopted the Volstead Act in 1920 to provide for its enforcement. Right, a Philadelphia safety director smashes a barrel of beer. (Library of Congress)

Membership in the Ku Klux Klan, a secret anti-black, ▶ anti-Catholic, anti-Semitic organization that sometimes resorted to arson and lynching to promote its doctrine of white supremacy, reached an all-time high during the 1920s. The Klan could boast some three million members in 1924. Here, new members are received during a nighttime meeting. The Klan disbanded in 1944 but emerged again two years later, focusing on Communism and civil rights issues.

(Library of Congress)

During the 1920s, the automobile became widely avail-able and more affordable than ever before. By the end of the decade, there were twenty-nine million cars on American roads. Right, a Ford coupe from 1923. ▶

(Library of Congress)

George Gershwin produced some of America's most popular music during the 1920s. He com-posed not only songs but also musical comedies, film scores, and the opera *Porgy and Bess*. Gershwin composed his first concert composition, *Rhapsody in Blue*, which combined jazz elements and classical piano, in 1924.

(Movie Star News) ▼

When President Harding died while still in office in 1923, Vice President Calvin Coolidge became president. In the election of 1924, Coolidge easily defeated Democrat John W. Davis. (Library of Congress) ▼

American physicist Robert H. Goddard ▶ pioneered the development of rocket power. Goddard successfully fired the world's first liquid-fueled rocket from the farm of a relative near Auburn, Massachusetts, on March 16, 1926. Right, Goddard poses with an experimental rocket.

(National Air and Space Museum)

◀ Trumpet player Louis "Satchmo" Armstrong, the first well-known male jazz singer, helped to make jazz a popular music style. Both playing and singing, Armstrong made some of his most famous recordings, including "West End Blues," from 1925 to 1928.

(Movie Star News)

On May 9, 1926, naval officer and aviator Richard E. Byrd and his pilot-mechanic Floyd Bennett made headlines as the first to fly an airplane over the North Pole. Considered dashing and brave by people of the day, Byrd was hailed as a national hero, given a ticker-tape parade in New York City, and welcomed at the White House.

(AP/Wide World)
▼

Babe Ruth, called the Sultan of Swat, hit sixty home runs in the 1927 baseball season, setting a record that stood for thirty-four years. One of the most popular players the game has known, Ruth helped lead the New York Yankees to four world championships. (Baseball Nostalgia) ▶

Before 1927, the movies were silent; the film itself had no sound to accompany the action. When actors spoke, the words they said were seen on the screen. That changed in 1927, when *The Jazz Singer*, the first full-length movie with sound, was released. It starred singer Al Jolson, who performed in blackface, that is, he was made up to look like a black entertainer. Mary McAvoy was his costar. (Movie Star News)

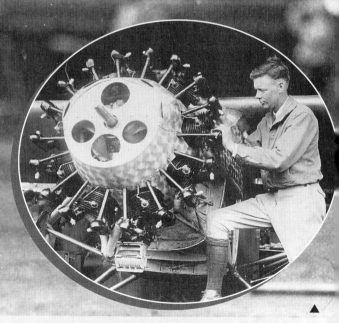

Charles Lindbergh astonished the world in 1927 by making the first nonstop flight across the Atlantic Ocean in the *Spirit of Saint Louis*, flying from New York to Paris in thirty-three and a half hours. Called the Lone Eagle and Lucky Lindy, the aviator received a tumultuous welcome on his return to the United States and was awarded the Congressional Medal of Honor. (Library of Congress)

▲
When the first coast-to-coast passenger air service began in the summer of 1929, passengers flew in a Ford Trimotor (a pair of which are pictured here), operated by Transcontinental Air Transport. Since there was no completed system of radio navigational aids across the country, part of the journey had to be made by train. The first plane-train coast-to-coast trip took forty-eight hours. (National Air and Space Museum)

▲
Police on horseback help to control the anxious crowd outside the New York Stock Exchange in October 1929. On October 29 that year, the blackest day in stock market history, stock prices plunged, helping to trigger a long and harsh economic crisis.

(AP/Wide World)

Herbert Hoover, elected in ▶ 1928, became the third consecutive Republican president of the United States (following Calvin Coolidge and Warren G. Harding). With prosperous times, most voters saw no reason to vote the Republicans out of power. (Library of Congress)

THE 1930s

New Deal Democracy

"WE IN AMERICA TODAY are nearer to the final triumph over poverty than ever before in the history of any land," Herbert Hoover declared in August 1928. "The poorhouse is vanishing from among us."

Herbert Hoover, elected president in 1928, was wrong. Only fifteen months after he made that statement, the United States tumbled into one of the worst economic crises in history — the Great Depression.

Americans had suffered through hard times before. But no depression lasted so long and touched so many Americans so harshly. Triggered by the stock market crash and financial panic of October 1929, the Great Depression continued through the 1930s. Years of standstill, the decade has been called.

More than 15 million people (out of a population of 123 million) were unemployed during the depths of the Depression. Businesses suffered huge losses. Banks by the thousands failed, and millions of people lost their savings and their homes. Family farms had to be sold. People went hungry.

The widespread poverty and misery forced Americans to rethink the role of the federal government in dealing with the nation's economic problems. As a result, a new emphasis came to be placed on the principles of social justice.

President Hoover resisted the idea of getting the federal government involved in the lives of Americans. Change came with the election of Franklin D. Roosevelt in 1932 as the nation's thirty-second president. Roosevelt offered what he called the New Deal, a wide range of domestic programs meant to bring relief, stimulate economic recovery, and prevent similar downturns in the future.

Laws were passed to create public works projects to furnish temporary jobs for the unemployed. Federal insurance protected workers' savings. Social Security provided financial benefits for the unemployed and older citizens. The fine arts were not overlooked. New Deal projects employed thousands of musicians, writers, painters, and sculptors.

Roosevelt's New Deal programs did not end the Great Depression, which lingered into the 1940s. His greatest contribution may have been on an emotional and psychological level. With his confidence and optimism, the president created a climate of hope at a time of little hope.

In a decade dominated by the economic crisis and its horrors, cultural life often focused on escape fantasies. Hollywood provided everything from *Frankenstein* (1931) and *King Kong* (1933) to *Gone With the Wind* (1939) and *The Wizard of Oz* (1939). Radio was an important source of entertainment. Bingo nights and the game of Monopoly zoomed in popularity. Dance marathons became popular, too. Such diversions allowed people to put aside their troubles and burdens, at least temporarily.

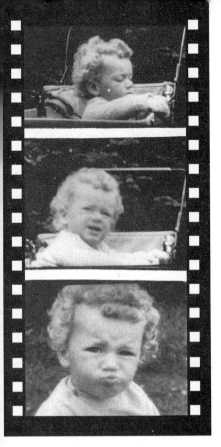

◄ The nation was horrified and deeply saddened by the kidnapping and murder of the twenty-month-old son of aviation hero, Charles Lindbergh, and his wife, Anne Morrow, in 1932. Bruno Richard Hauptmann was convicted of the crime. Although he proclaimed he was innocent, Hauptmann was executed four years later. (AP/Wide World)

When construction was completed on ▶ the Empire State Building in New York City in 1931, the structure, at 110 stories, 1,250 feet, ranked as the tallest building in the world. The Empire State Building held the distinction of being the world's tallest until 1972, when it fell into second place behind the World Trade Center. (AP/Wide World)

◄ The Great Depression triggered an unprecedented level of suffering in the United States. Many people found it necessary to stand in breadlines for food. Left, an early 1930s breadline in New York City. (Library of Congress)

In the summer of 1932, some twenty thousand out-of-work veterans of World War I went to Washington, D.C., to demand that Congress pay the "bonus" that had been promised to them. About two thousand marchers lived in tents and shacks while they waited for congressional action. After the marchers clashed with local police, President Hoover called on federal troops to rout them with bayonets, tear gas, and tanks. (AP/Wide World)

▲ During the presidential election campaign of 1932, Democratic candidate Franklin D. Roosevelt, who promised a New Deal for the American people, scored a crushing victory over President Hoover. Above, Roosevelt shakes hands with admirers, following a campaign speech. (Franklin D. Roosevelt Library)

▲ When Franklin D. Roosevelt became president in 1933, he named Frances Perkins to be secretary of labor. The first woman to serve as a cabinet member, Perkins helped draft much of the New Deal legislation that was meant to benefit workers and the unemployed.

(Franklin D. Roosevelt Library)

Some Americans who had lost their jobs and homes built crude shelters out of packing crates and sheet metal, creating encampments within major cities. Since many held President Herbert Hoover to blame for the crisis, they called shantytowns like this one in Seattle, Washington, Hoovervilles.

(AP/Wide World)

Four-year-old dimpled and golden-curled Shirley Temple sang and tap-danced her way to motion picture stardom in *Stand Up and Cheer* and *Little Miss Marker*, both released in 1934. She made twenty-five movies during the 1930s, becoming the decade's biggest box-office attraction. Temple later served as the U.S. representative to the United Nations, ambassador to Ghana, and ambassador to Czechoslovakia. She now lives in California.

(Movie Star News)

A major sea disaster occurred early in September 1934 when the cruise ship *Morro Castle*, weighing eleven thousand tons and bound for New York City from Havana, Cuba, was swept by a blaze that turned the ship's interior into a roaring furnace. The fire claimed the lives of 134 passengers and crew members. Stiff winds drove the ship toward the New Jersey shore off Asbury Park, where thousands lined the shore to view the smoking hulk.

(AP/Wide World)

Eleanor Roosevelt, the wife of President Franklin D. Roosevelt and a tireless worker for social causes, including racial equality, helped during her husband's years in office to expand the role of the First Lady. She held press conferences, wrote a daily newspaper column, and urged the president to include more minorities and women in New Deal programs.

(AP/Wide World)

Jesse Owens was the sensation of the 1936 Olympic Games, held in Berlin, Germany, winning four gold medals for the United States. Owens broke Olympic records in the 200-meter dash, long jump, and as part of the 4 x 100-meter relay. He also tied the record for the 100-meter dash. (AP/Wide World)

◀ Baseball opened its Hall of Fame and Museum in Cooperstown, New York, in 1936 to honor outstanding players, managers, umpires, and others connected with the game. Five players were elected to Hall of Fame membership that year, including Ty Cobb (pictured here), one of baseball's all-time great hitters; Babe Ruth, the legendary home-run hero; and Honus Wagner, perhaps the finest shortstop of all time. (Baseball Nostalgia)

As if the Great Depression was not enough, much of the Great Plains suffered from frequent dust storms during the 1930s. In the Dakotas, Nebraska, Kansas, Oklahoma, Texas, and parts of Colorado and New Mexico, torrid winds swept across parched fields, creating great clouds of dust and darkening afternoon skies. Thousands died of "dust pneumonia." This scene depicts buried machinery on a farm near Dallas, South Dakota. (National Archives)

Movies enjoyed a golden age during the 1930s. Studios turned out a record number of films, including some of the most memorable of all time. One such triumph was *Snow White and the Seven Dwarfs*, Walt Disney's first feature-length animated motion picture. (Movie Star News)
▼

The *Hindenburg* was the biggest airship ever built. It began service in 1936, providing luxury air transport between the United States and Germany. On May 6, 1937, as it was maneuvering to land at Lakehurst, New Jersey, a spectacular explosion racked the silvery aircraft. Thirty-six of the *Hindenburg's* ninety-seven passengers and crew members died in the disaster. (AP/Wide World)

Joe Louis (left), known as the Brown Bomber, won the heavyweight boxing championship on June 22, 1937, knocking out James J. Braddock. A heroic figure to millions of black Americans of the 1930s and 1940s, Louis held the title until 1949, when he retired. His reign as champion was the longest in the history of the heavyweight division. Here, Louis struggles with Abe Simon in a championship match in Madison Square Garden in New York City in 1942. He knocked out Simon in the fourth round.

(AP/Wide World)

Adapted from the classic children's story by ▶
L. Frank Baum, *The Wizard of Oz* made its
debut as a motion picture in 1939. Among
the most endearing films ever produced, the
musical fantasy featured Bert Lahr as the
Cowardly Lion; Jack Haley as the Tin
Woodman; sixteen-year-old Judy Garland as
the Kansas girl who is transported to Oz;
and Ray Bolger as the Scarecrow.
(Movie Star News)

A clarinetist and bandleader, Benny Goodman helped to
develop a new type of music during the 1930s called
swing, a smooth-flowing style of jazz. He is often credited
as being the first important bandleader to integrate white
and black musicians in performance groups. (AP/Wide World)
▼

▲
After Charles Lindbergh, the greatest aviator of the day was Amelia Earhart,
who, in 1932, became the first woman to fly the Atlantic Ocean alone. On June
1, 1937, Earhart and navigator Freddie Noonan left Miami, Florida, to attempt
an around-the-world flight. On June 29, they landed at Lae, New Guinea, and
two days later took off for tiny Howland Island in the central Pacific Ocean.
Their plane seemingly vanished. No trace of Earhart, Noonan, or their aircraft
has ever been found, creating one of the most enduring mysteries of the
twentieth century. (AP/Wide World)

In a decade in which the movies flourished, *Gone With the Wind* ▶ was hailed as Hollywood's greatest triumph. Based on Margaret Mitchell's novel, the Civil War masterpiece starred Clark Gable as Rhett Butler and Vivian Leigh as a fiery daughter of the Confederacy, Scarlett O'Hara. *Gone With the Wind* won a record ten Oscars and shattered box-office records. (Movie Star News)

◀ As the 1930s ended, war erupted in Europe. On September 1, 1939, Germany invaded Poland. Here, a London newsdealer displays word of the event. World War II officially began when Great Britain and France immediately declared war on the aggressors. "The nation will remain a neutral nation," President Roosevelt declared shortly after the war broke out. Nevertheless, people in the United States worried that sooner or later the nation would be forced to choose sides in the conflict. (Archive Photos)

▲ When the Daughters of the American Revolution refused to give black opera singer Marian Anderson permission to sing at Constitution Hall in Washington, D.C., First Lady Eleanor Roosevelt, along with Interior Secretary Harold Ickes, protested and helped secure government approval for Anderson to sing on the steps of the Lincoln Memorial. The Easter Sunday concert drew an enormous crowd, estimated at seventy-five thousand. Looking back, some historians call it the first modern civil rights demonstration.

(Library of Congress)

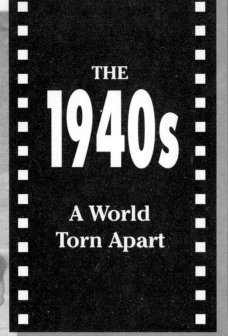

THE
1940s

A World Torn Apart

IT WAS THE MOST TERRIBLE DAY IN American history. At 7:55 A.M. on December 7, 1941, a sunny Sunday, hundreds of Japanese bombers and fighter planes launched a surprise attack on the United States naval base at Pearl Harbor in the Hawaiian Islands. Eighteen ships were sunk or badly damaged, more than two hundred planes were destroyed, and 2,323 servicemen were killed.

The next day, at the urging of President Franklin D. Roosevelt, Congress approved a declaration of war against Japan. Within a week, Congress also declared war on Japan's allies, Germany and Italy. For the second time in less than twenty-five years, the United States was involved in a world war.

World War II, as it came to be called, had officially begun earlier, on September 1, 1939, when Germany launched a full-scale invasion of Poland. After a quick victory there, the German army occupied Denmark and Norway. Before 1940 ended, Germany conquered Holland, Belgium, and France, driving to the English Channel and leaving England standing alone.

The United States was transformed by the war. From the day Pearl Harbor was bombed until world peace arrived in 1945, Americans saw their lives pulled apart. The remaining years of the decade were spent trying to put their lives back together. But nothing was ever the same.

With the war's end, Americans worried that hard times would return — that factory jobs would disappear without the enormous sums of money that had been spent on defense. It didn't happen. A surge of consumer demand after the war set the stage for years of broad-based prosperity. "People wanted stuff" is the way one observer put it. Suburbs sprang up everywhere. Big cars rolled off Detroit's assembly lines by the millions. And during the late 1940s and early 1950s the United States saw the explosive growth of a new and powerful medium of mass communication: television.

Millions of former servicemen and -women took advantage of the GI Bill of Rights, which provided funds for college tuition and living expenses. It also guaranteed loans for the purchase of homes, farms, and businesses.

Before the war, most Americans had struggled. By the end of the decade, millions of formerly poor people were becoming a vast middle class.

Nevertheless, peace and harmony proved elusive in postwar America. Within two years after the end of World War II, growing tension between the United States and the Soviet Union led to the Cold War. Despite their new homes, shiny cars, and college degrees, Americans faced troubled times and an uncertain future.

The 1940s began with eight million Americans out of work. The Depression had dragged on for so long that many people thought it was never going to end. During the winter of 1940, more than six hundred men a day ate and slept at the House of Hospitality in Pittsburgh, Pennsylvania. (AP/Wide World)

Ted Williams of the Boston ▶
Red Sox, who had a lifetime
batting average of .344,
became the last baseball
player to average more than
.400 when he hit .406 in
1941. Williams won six
batting titles in his fourteen-
year career with the Boston
team and hit 521 career
home runs. He joined
baseball's Hall of Fame
in 1966.

(Baseball Nostalgia)

In 1940, Franklin D. Roosevelt did what no president
had ever done before: He ran for a third term. He was
an easy winner. (Franklin D. Roosevelt Library)
▼

In 1932, with the Great Depression at its
worst, more than half of the blacks in the
South were unemployed. Federal or state
relief that did happen to be available
almost always went to whites. One result
was a vast migration of blacks from the
Deep South to northern cities. Here, a
family from Florida prepares to leave for
New Jersey in 1940.

(Library of Congress)

Hysterical young female fans, called bobby-soxers, helped to make Frank Sinatra the singing sensation of the 1940s. That popularity was not equaled until the arrival of the Beatles in the 1960s. Sinatra also enjoyed a long-running career as a Hollywood actor and won an Academy Award for his performance in *From Here to Eternity.*

(Movie Star News)

Sugar, butter, meat, gasoline — and automobile tires — were in short supply during the war. The government responded by limiting the purchase of such items through a nationwide system of rationing. (National Archives)
▼

▲
Following Japan's attack on Pearl Harbor, President Roosevelt and his advisers, fearing that Americans of Japanese ancestry might assist a West Coast invasion by Japan, forcibly relocated more than 100,000 Japanese-American citizens to internment camps. This photo pictures members of the Mochida family as they await a bus that is to take them to an internment camp.

(National Archives)

For the United States, World War II began when the Japanese bombed Pearl Harbor, Hawaii, on December 7, 1941. The attack crippled the nation's Pacific fleet. (U.S. Navy)

With so many men serving in the armed forces, millions of women went to work in defense industries. Right, women workers turn out clear plastic noses for fighter planes at a Douglas Aircraft plant in Long Beach, California. (National Archives) ▶

Allied forces under the command of General Dwight D. Eisenhower landed in Morocco and Algeria in North Africa in November 1942 and won important victories in areas under German control. Below, U.S. troops on the beach at Fedala, Morocco, after going ashore. (AP/Wide World)

▼

The ability of the United States to produce huge quantities of weapons and everything else needed for the war effort was a decisive factor in the eventual Allied victory. This shipbuilding plant in Los Angeles was capable of launching a new vessel every thirty-six hours. (AP/Wide World)

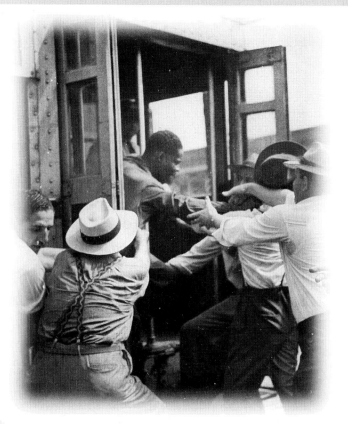

On June 6, 1944 — D Day — Allied forces under the command of General Dwight D. Eisenhower launched an invasion of Hitler's "Fortress Europe," landing troops at several locations along the Normandy coast of France. Above, Eisenhower addresses paratroopers from the United States in the hours before the invasion.

(Dwight D. Eisenhower Library)

The migration of large numbers of blacks to industrial cities of the North created race relations problems. Detroit experienced more tension than any other city. On June 21, 1943, serious race riots erupted there. President Roosevelt, declaring a state of emergency, sent six thousand soldiers to patrol the city and bring peace. Above, a black male is dragged from a streetcar near downtown Detroit during the evening of June 26. (AP/Wide World)

Early in 1944, American forces attacked the Japanese-held Marshall Islands in the central Pacific. Here, marines under sniper fire dig in on the beach at Roi Island. In the background, marine demolition specialists destroy Japanese shore installations.

(U.S. Marine Corps)

A signpost put up by U.S. soldiers on Leyte Island in the Philippines names places at home they remembered and missed. (National Archives)

Troops in the southwest Pacific under the command of General Douglas MacArthur went on the offensive against the Japanese early in 1943. As part of the campaign, MacArthur's forces landed on the Philippine island of Leyte in October 1944 and invaded Luzon, also in the Philippines, in January 1945. Above, MacArthur (in sunglasses) goes ashore in Luzon on January 22, 1945. (National Archives)

An American howitzer shells German forces retreating near Carentan, France, on July 11, 1944, almost five weeks after D Day. (National Archives)

D Day, involving almost three million troops and four thousand vessels, was the largest amphibious operation in history. Here, hundreds of U.S. assault troops move from their landing craft to what was called Omaha Beach in northern France on June 6, 1944. (National Archives)

◀ Enormous fleets of four-engined B-29 Superfortresses, the biggest bomber of World War II, began pounding Japanese cities in the early months of 1945. Osaka, Kobe, Nagoya, and huge sections of Tokyo were reduced to ashes. (National Archives)

▲

In February 1945, the "Big Three," Britain's prime minister Winston S. Churchill, President Franklin D. Roosevelt, and Soviet leader Joseph Stalin, met in the Soviet Crimea at Yalta to discuss the postwar world. Some basic differences between the three men were never resolved. The next time the Allied leaders met, in July 1945, only Stalin would be in power. (National Archives)

◀ Associated Press photographer Joe Rosenthal took this historic photo of U.S. Marines raising the flag at Mount Suribachi on Iwo Jima, one of a chain of islands in the South Pacific, on February 19, 1945, near the end of World War II.

(AP/Wide World)

Harry S. Truman became president on the death of Franklin D. Roosevelt. Above, Truman, his wife and daughter at his side, during oath-taking ceremonies at the White House.
(Harry S. Truman Library)

Mourners express their sorrow and pain as Roosevelt's funeral procession travels the streets of the nation's capital. (Franklin D. Roosevelt Library)

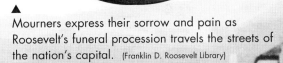

On April 12, 1945, less than three months after being inaugurated for a fourth term, President Roosevelt suffered a massive stroke and died while at his vacation retreat at Warm Springs, Georgia. Here, Roosevelt's funeral procession makes its way from Washington, D.C.'s Union Station to the White House. Judged one of the nation's strongest presidents, Roosevelt held office for twelve years, thirty-nine days.
(Franklin D. Roosevelt Library)

▲
The campaign by the Nazis — the members of the National Socialist Party, which controlled Germany — to wipe out the Jews of Europe during World War II was one of the great tragedies of world history. Jews and others, including Poles, homosexuals, and Communists, were rounded up, held in concentration camps, then murdered. The death toll reached ten million, including six million Jews. These are starved prisoners from a concentration camp at Ebensee, Austria, liberated by American forces in May 1945. (National Archives)

Although the war in Europe had ended, the war in the Pacific continued. On August 6, 1945, a U.S. Superfortress dropped an atomic bomb on the Japanese city of Hiroshima. About 75,000 Japanese were killed instantly and 100,000 injured. Two days later, the Soviet Union declared war on Japan. The following day, August 9, the United States dropped a second bomb, this time over the city of Nagasaki (below). On September 2, the stunned Japanese government formally surrendered.
(National Archives)
▼

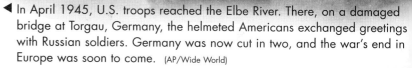

◀ In April 1945, U.S. troops reached the Elbe River. There, on a damaged bridge at Torgau, Germany, the helmeted Americans exchanged greetings with Russian soldiers. Germany was now cut in two, and the war's end in Europe was soon to come. (AP/Wide World)

◀ Part of the waving, cheering crowd in New York City's Times Square that greeted reports of Japan's surrender and the war's end on August 14, 1945. (AP/Wide World)

A massive, joyous crowd in New York City's Times Square celebrates the end of the war in Europe — V-E Day — on May 8, 1945. (AP/Wide World)

A cemetery in France for U.S. soldiers who died in the invasion of Normandy. World War II took the lives of some 322,000 Americans. (AP/Wide World)

▼

In 1945, delegates from fifty nations developed a plan for an international organization to work for world peace and security, to be called the United Nations. All fifty nations signed the charter and more than a hundred other nations have since joined. Here, the United Nations headquarters in New York City. (George Sullivan)

When Jackie Robinson joined the Brooklyn Dodgers in 1947, he became the first black player in major league baseball. Despite insults and threats, Robinson carved out an exceptional career, becoming Rookie of the Year in 1947 and winning the Most Valuable Player award in 1949. In 1962, Robinson became the first black player to enter baseball's Hall of Fame. More important than his many baseball achievements, Robinson spearheaded the breaking of the color barrier in American professional sports.
(Baseball Nostalgia)

In 1946, two engineers at the University of Pennsylvania's Moore School of Electrical Engineering, John Prosper Eckert, Jr., and John William Mauchly, built the first general-purpose electronic digital computer. Called ENIAC, for Electronic Numerical Integrator and Computer, the huge U-shaped machine contained 18,000 vacuum tubes and 1,500 relays, occupied more than 1,500 square feet, and weighed more than thirty tons.
(University of Pennsylvania Archives)

One of the worst disasters in American history took place on April 16, 1947, in the harbor of Texas City, Texas, when the French freighter *Grandcamp* caught fire, causing its ammonium-nitrate fertilizer cargo to explode. As a result, a series of explosions was set off and fires swept through the city, bringing death to 576 people. Here, a general view of the scene on April 17 as fires continued to rage.
(AP/Wide World)

On October 14, 1947, U.S. Air Force Captain Charles "Chuck" Yeager, flying the bullet-shaped Bell X-1 over the Mojave Desert near Muroc Dry Lake, California, became the first to fly faster than the speed of sound (760 miles per hour at sea level). (AP/Wide World)

In the presidential election of 1948, newspapers, pollsters, and politicians expected Republican Thomas Dewey to defeat President Truman. Final returns gave Truman the victory in one of the biggest political upsets in American history. Above, Truman chuckles at an erroneous announcement of his defeat in an early edition of the *Chicago Tribune*. (AP/Wide World)

Experiments in broadcasting pictures along with sound had begun during the 1920s. But World War II interrupted television's development. After the war, the medium experienced phenomenal growth. In 1946, there were only seventeen thousand television sets in the United States. By 1953, two-thirds of all Americans had TVs. Above, the New York plant of the United States Television Manufacturing Corporation in 1947. (AP/Wide World)

During the 1940s, people began to report seeing lights or disk-shaped objects in the sky that had no obvious explanation. In 1947, the press coined the term "flying saucers" to describe these sightings. (AP/Wide World)

During the early years of the Cold War, the United States and the Soviet Union wrangled over the city of Berlin, which, at the time, lay deep within Soviet-controlled East Germany and was divided into four occupation zones: American, British, French, and Soviet. The Soviets, in an effort to gain complete control of Berlin, cut off supplies of food and fuel to the city in 1948. The United States and Great Britain responded with a massive airlift. Every day for almost ten months, American and British cargo planes like the one pictured above landed in West Berlin, sometimes as frequently as one per minute. The airlift succeeded in causing the Soviets to lift the blockade on May 17, 1949. (AP/Wide World)

Milton Berle was one reason television enjoyed such rapid growth ▶ during the 1940s. His hour-long show, originally called *The Texaco Star Theater*, which had its premiere on September 21, 1948, was television's first big hit. People who didn't own TV sets went out and bought them to be able to watch Uncle Miltie. Berle later came to be known as Mr. Television. (AP/Wide World)

THE 1950s

Cold War, Hot War

THE 1950S WERE ONCE LOOKED upon as being uninteresting and drab. It was a postwar decade, and veterans of World War II set much of the agenda. They were concerned about their careers, their families, and their homes in the fast-growing suburbs.

On their fuzzy black-and-white television sets, people watched *Father Knows Best*, *Ozzie and Harriet*, and *I Love Lucy*. Lots of fun but not much excitement.

Dwight D. Eisenhower, who was president for much of the decade, had a lulling effect upon the nation. He made Americans feel comfortable. "The great problem of America today," said Eisenhower, "is to take that straight road down the middle."

But in recent years, people have changed their minds about the 1950s. They now realize that the decade was anything but dull. Important events took place; important trends were born.

The Cold War, the relentless hostility between the United States and the Soviet Union, got very tense during this decade. In 1950, the Cold War became hot. The Korean War began on June 25, 1950, when troops from Communist-controlled North Korea invaded South Korea. The United Nations asked its members to give military aid to the South Koreans, and sixteen nations sent troops. It was the United States, however, that provided most of the military manpower and equipment, ninety percent of it, in fact. Few protested; fewer resisted. The war

lasted three years, took the lives of more than thirty-three thousand Americans, and resulted in a cease-fire line to serve as a border between North and South Korea.

At about the time that the Korean War was winding down, the Civil Rights movement was heating up. In 1954, the Supreme Court ruled that segregated education was unconstitutional. In 1955, it ordered segregated school districts to integrate "with all deliberate speed." The legal basis for the American system of separation had been overturned.

The 1950s also saw the rise of the teenager. Before World War II, a child was a child until he or she became a grown-up. But by the late 1950s, teenagers were a distinct group. They had their own music, rock 'n' roll, and Elvis Presley, one of the first rock stars. They had their own movies. *Rebel Without a Cause*, starring James Dean, was one. They had their own style of dress: pedal pushers, pompadours, and ponytails.

Some of the words and terms that came into use during the 1950s (according to Lois and Alan Gordon in *American Chronicle*) included: H-bomb, split-level, name-dropper, fallout, integration, DNA, hip, funky, automated, junk mail, discount house, hot rod, hot line, cookout, put-on, and Third World. A decade that originated all those expressions can't be considered dull and drab.

▼ On July 17, 1950, when the United States was involved in the Cold War with the Soviet Union and an undeclared shooting war in Korea, Julius Rosenberg and his wife, Ethel, were arrested and later convicted of giving information to the Soviet Union about U.S. nuclear weapons. Both were sentenced to death. Although the couple denied their guilt and many believed their sentence to be unjust, the Rosenbergs were executed, becoming the first U.S. citizens ever put to death during peacetime for espionage.

(AP/Wide World)

▲ From 1951 through 1957, *I Love Lucy* was among television's top-rated programs. It eventually won acclaim as one of the most popular TV comedies of all time. The show starred the comic actors Lucille Ball as a zany housewife and Desi Arnaz, her husband, as a bandleader. (Movie Star News)

◄ The Korean War began on June 24, 1950, when troops from Communist-dominated North Korea invaded South Korea. Here, paratroopers of the 187th Regimental Combat Team drift earthward from C-119s. Their mission was to cut off North Korean units retreating south of Munsan, Korea, in March 1951. (National Archives)

Private Edward Wilson of the 24th Infantry Regiment, wounded in the leg during combat near the front lines in Korea, waits to be evacuated to an aid station. ►

(National Archives)

Edward Teller and other U.S. scientists exploded the first hydrogen bomb on Eniwetok, a tiny coral island in the western Pacific, on November 1, 1952. Hydrogen bombs, also called thermonuclear bombs, were described as being hundreds, even thousands, of times more powerful than atomic bombs. (AP/Wide World)

▲ Actress Marilyn Monroe, a favorite of the public and the media, rose to stardom with several film successes in the 1950s, including *Gentlemen Prefer Blondes* (1953), *The Seven Year Itch* (1955), and *Some Like It Hot* (1959). A year after her final film, *The Misfits* (1961), Monroe, at age thirty-six, died of an overdose of sleeping pills. (Movie Star News)

◄ Author Ernest Hemingway won the 1953 Pulitzer Prize for his novel *The Old Man and the Sea* and received the Nobel Prize for Literature in 1954. Hemingway's style, with its crisp and simple language and finely detailed descriptions, had influenced a generation and more of writers. (AP/Wide World)

▼ Television's *The Mickey Mouse Club*, featuring the Mouseketeers, below, made its debut as a weekday program for kids in 1955. Disneyland, Disney's first amusement park, also opened that year in California. (AP/Wide World)

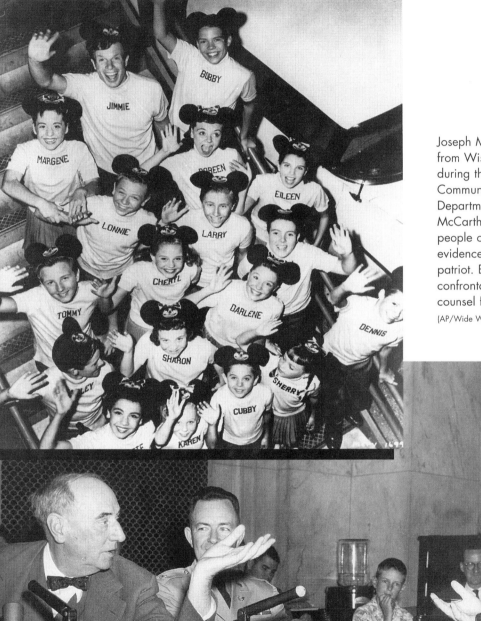

Joseph McCarthy, a Republican senator from Wisconsin, gained national attention during the early 1950s after charging that Communists had infiltrated the State Department and the U.S. Army. Although McCarthy was denounced for accusing people of disloyalty without supporting evidence, many Americans hailed him as a patriot. Below, McCarthy (right) in a confrontation with Joseph Welch, chief counsel for the army, during the hearings. (AP/Wide World) ▼

In 1955, the federal government announced the availability of a safe and effective killer-virus vaccine for the prevention of poliomyelitis, a frequently crippling disease that primarily struck infants and young children. Left, Dr. Jonas Salk, the American research scientist who had developed the serum, gives an autograph. (AP/Wide World)

In his second term, President Dwight D. Eisenhower ordered federal troops to Little Rock, Arkansas, on September 24, 1957, when the state defied a court order to integrate the all-white Central High School. Outside the school, an angry mob formed, determined to prevent integration. Above, a National Guardsman points the way to Elizabeth Echford. (AP/Wide World)

In Montgomery, Alabama, in the early 1950s, blacks and whites were segregated on city buses. On December 1, 1955, when Rosa Parks, a black woman who lived there, refused to give up her seat to a white passenger, she was arrested. Here, Parks is fingerprinted by a deputy sheriff after her arrest. In the months following the incident, Dr. Martin Luther King, Jr., pastor of a Montgomery church at the time, led a bus boycott that eventually was successful in ending segregation on Montgomery city buses. (AP/Wide World)

After colliding with the Swedish ocean liner *Stockholm* in thick fog off Nantucket Island on the night of July 26, 1956, the Italian ocean liner *Andrea Doria* overturned and sank. More than fifty people died.
(AP/Wide World)

◀ Elvis Presley, whose tough, rebellious manner appealed to teenagers, burst upon the scene during the 1950s. Presley's first hit single, "Heartbreak Hotel," was issued in 1956. Other chart-toppers followed, including "Don't Be Cruel," "Hound Dog," and "Love Me Tender." Also in 1956, Presley's first motion picture, *Love Me Tender*, was released. He went on to appear in thirty-two other movies. Later regarded as the single most influential figure in the history of rock music, Presley died in 1977 at the age of forty-two.
(AP/Wide World)

On August 3, 1958, at precisely 11:15 P.M., the submarine *Nautilus*, cruising far beneath the polar ice pack, became the first vessel in history to pass under the North Pole. The *Nautilus* was, in fact, the first vessel ever to reach the pole. (U.S. Navy)

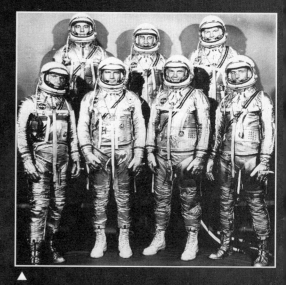

On October 1, 1958, Congress established the National Aeronautics and Space Agency (NASA) to direct the nation's ventures beyond the earth's atmosphere. Project Mercury, a program to put a man into space, was announced six months later. Project Mercury astronauts included, front row, left to right, Walter M. Schirra, Jr., Donald K. "Deke" Slayton, John H. Glenn, Jr., and M. Scott Carpenter; back row, Alan B. Shepard, Jr., Virgil I. "Gus" Grissom, and L. Gordon Cooper. (NASA)

The world was thrust suddenly into the Space Age on October 4, 1957, when the Soviet Union launched *Sputnik* (Russian for "traveler"), the first artificial satellite. The United States responded on January 31, 1958, when a Jupiter C rocket (shown here) lifted into the air carrying an Explorer satellite. (AP/Wide World)

The No. 1 fad of the 1950s was the hula hoop, a plastic circle about three feet around that was available in many different colors. Kids spun the hoops mostly around their hips, but also around their necks, knees, and ankles. (AP/Wide World)

▲
During the summer of 1959, Nikita Khrushchev became the first Soviet leader to travel across the United States. Above (left), Khrushchev holds an ear of corn grown on a farm in Coon Rapids, Iowa; (right) he prepares to eat a hot dog in Des Moines.

(Collection of Alex Tabourin)

At a White House get-together to celebrate Alaskan statehood, Alaska's governor Michael A. Stepovich holds an Anchorage newspaper that proclaims the good news. At Stepovich's left is President Dwight D. Eisenhower; at his right, Secretary of the Interior Fred Seaton. The nation's forty-ninth state, Alaska officially joined the union on January 3, 1959. For Hawaii, the fiftieth state, the date was August 21, 1959. ▶

(Library of Congress)

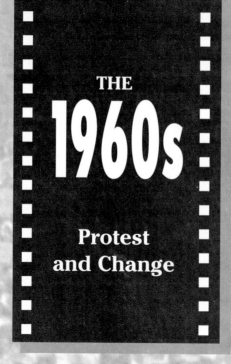

THE 1960s

Protest and Change

CHANGE. THAT'S WHAT THE 1960s were about. Social change, political change, changes that would have a deep effect on the lives of every American.

The changes did not come easily. There were riots in 130 American cities during the 1960s, takeovers of college campuses, and rage from antiwar protestors.

There were the assassinations of President John F. Kennedy, Malcolm X, the Reverend Martin Luther King, Jr., and Senator Robert F. Kennedy.

The decade that was to produce so much trauma and turmoil began on an optimistic note. President Kennedy, elected in 1960, had youth and style. Americans were charmed by him. But he was able to do little to change the existing state of things.

Meanwhile, there were rumblings — "sit-ins" to integrate restaurants and "freedom rides" to integrate interstate buses. Thousands of civil rights workers fanned out through the South, demanding an end to segregation and a greater role for blacks in the political process.

After President Kennedy was murdered in Dallas in 1963, Vice President Lyndon B. Johnson became president. Ambitious and energetic, Johnson accomplished more in his first hundred days than Kennedy had achieved in almost three years — a tax cut, a foreign aid bill, and a Civil Rights Act that prohibited racial discrimination in restaurants, theaters, and other places of "public accommodation." Johnson then declared a war on poverty and set out to shape what was called "the Great Society."

But President Johnson's grand plans were undercut by what was happening in Vietnam. In 1965, when South Vietnam came close to collapse, and with many Americans believing that the United States should stop aggression and prevent the spread of Communism, Johnson stepped up the nation's involvement in Vietnam.

As the war kept getting hotter and hotter, young people began to protest. They staged marches and sit-ins, ransacked draft boards, and torched campus ROTC (Reserve Officers Training Corps) buildings.

There was great turbulence among blacks, too. The political gains of the Civil Rights movement raised blacks' hopes. But many were discouraged because there was no improvement in their economic status. The frustration helped to trigger devastating urban riots. Los Angeles, New York, Newark, and scores of other cities were victimized in a frenzy of burning and looting.

By the end of the decade, the worst aspects of segregation had ended, and the United States had begun to withdraw its forces from Vietnam. Americans, however, were tired of turmoil and change. In the election of 1968, voters turned to Richard Nixon, of California, the son of hard-working middle-class parents, as a source of stability. But Nixon, as president, was to produce more years of crisis.

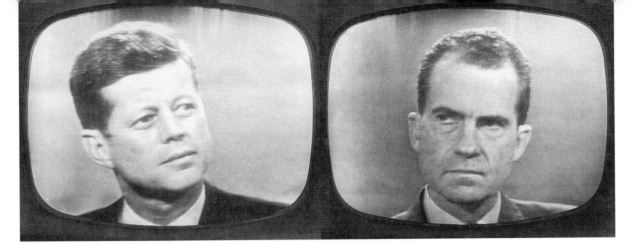

▲ When John F. Kennedy (left) ran against Richard Nixon in the 1960 presidential campaign, candidates faced each other in televised debates for the first time. Kennedy was warm, witty, and confident. Nixon often scowled and appeared uneasy. Seen by more than seventy million viewers, the debates helped Kennedy win what was an especially close election. (Library of Congress; *U.S. News & World Report* Collection)

◀ Roger Maris, an outfielder for the New York Yankees, made sports history when he hit sixty-one home runs in 1961, thereby breaking Babe Ruth's single-season home-run record of sixty, set in 1927. Maris's career in the major leagues spanned twelve seasons. Left, Maris poses with nineteen-year-old Sal Durante. Sitting in the right-field stands at Yankee Stadium, Durante caught the ball that Maris hit for his sixty-first home run. (AP/Wide World)

◀ In August 1963, more than 200,000 demonstrators gathered at the Lincoln Memorial in Washington for the greatest civil rights demonstration in the nation's history. Dr. Martin Luther King, Jr., aroused the huge crowd with his powerful "I Have a Dream" speech. (AP/Wide World)

▲ Upon taking office on January 20, 1961, John F. Kennedy, at forty-three, was the youngest man ever elected president. Above, Kennedy (left) and his vice president, Lyndon B. Johnson, a native Texan with thirty years of experience in politics, view the inauguration parade in Washington. (John F. Kennedy Library)

◀ John Glenn was acclaimed a national hero on February 20, 1962, when he became the first American to orbit the earth. A television audience of 100 million watched as the towering Atlas rocket carrying Glenn's *Friendship 7* space capsule lifted off from Cape Canaveral, Florida. (NASA)

In 1962, César Chávez, a Mexican-American migrant farmworker, organized ▶ the National Farm Workers Association, later named the United Farm Workers (UFW), in California. With the support of college students, churches, and civil rights organizations, the UFW organized a nationwide boycott of table grapes and lettuce to win recognition of the union and obtain increased wages and benefits for workers. Right, Chávez talks to striking workers in California's Salinas Valley in 1979. (AP/Wide World)

CHERRY PICKER

LAUNCH PAD WITH ERECTOR

LAUNCH PAD WITH ERECTOR

MISSILE READY BLDGS

What was perhaps the most dangerous crisis of the Cold War developed during 1962 when U.S. spy planes found clear evidence that the Soviet Union was building missile bases in Cuba. (Here, a Defense Department photograph of a missile base at Sagua la Grande in Cuba.) After a week of tense negotiations with the Soviets, President Kennedy announced that he planned to establish a naval and air blockade of Cuba to stop Soviet ships and planes from reaching the island. Work on the missile sites continued. Preparations were being made for U.S. planes to attack the sites. But on October 26, the Soviets relented, agreeing to remove the missile bases. The crisis was over. (AP/Wide World)

OXIDIZER VEHICLES

FUELING VEHICLES

In the spring of 1963, Martin Luther King, Jr., began a series of nonviolent civil rights marches and demonstrations in Birmingham, Alabama, to protest segregation in the city. Local officials responded with force, using fire hoses, electric cattle prods, tear gas, and attack dogs in an effort to break up the protests. Five demonstrators were injured, 250 were jailed.
(AP/Wide World)

Lyndon B. Johnson is sworn in as president before Judge ▶ Sarah Hughes in the cabin of *Air Force One*. Jacqueline Kennedy is at the right, and Johnson's wife, Lady Bird Johnson, at the left.
(AP/Wide World)

The world was shocked and deeply saddened when President Kennedy was assassinated in Dallas on November 22, 1963. He was riding in a motorcade in an open car, Mrs. Kennedy at his side, when the fatal bullets struck. This photograph, from a strip of motion picture film, depicts the president slumping against his wife moments after being shot.
(AP/Wide World)

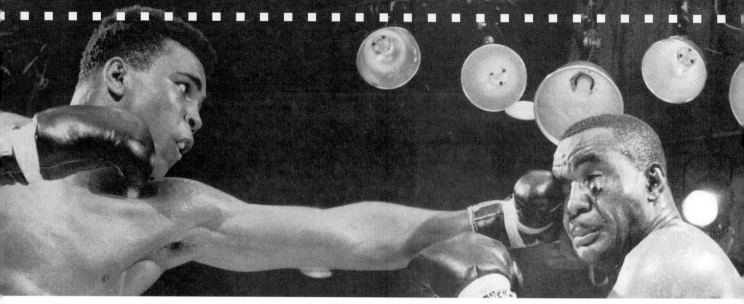

▲ Young Cassius Marcellus Clay (left) startled the sports world on February 26, 1964, when he scored a technical knockout over Sonny Liston to win the heavyweight boxing championship. After his conversion to Islam, Clay changed his name to Muhammad Ali. (AP/Wide World)

◀ Twenty-five-year-old Lee Harvey Oswald was arrested and charged with killing the president. The former U.S. Marine Corps sharpshooter was himself assassinated by Jack Ruby, a Dallas nightclub owner, two days later while being transferred to another jail. Ruby was charged with the murder, tried, and found guilty, but the verdict was later reversed. Left, Ruby steps out with gun in hand to make the fatal shot.

(Swann Galleries)

Mrs. Kennedy, with her daughter, Caroline, and son, ▶ John, attend funeral services for the president at St. Matthew's Cathedral in Washington. Robert Kennedy, the president's brother, is at her side.

(AP/Wide World)

Beatlemania swept the United States beginning in February 1964, when (from left) Paul McCartney, Ringo Starr, John Lennon, and George Harrison arrived from London on their first American visit. Here, the four wave to fans assembled below their Plaza Hotel window in New York City.

(AP/Wide World)

▼ In high spirits, the Reverend Martin Luther King, Jr. (left), and Malcolm X shake hands following a meeting on March 3, 1964, to discuss the Civil Rights Act, then before Congress. Signed into law by President Lyndon B. Johnson on July 2, 1964, the Civil Rights Act prohibited discrimination on the basis of race, religion, age, or sex.

(AP/Wide World)

After traveling around the country interviewing suburban housewives and ▶ mothers and asking them about their lives, Betty Friedan set down her findings in *The Feminine Mystique*, published in 1963. The book, which called upon women to fulfill "their unique possibilities as separate human beings," helped to give life to the feminist movement.

(AP/Wide World)

▲ During the "Freedom Summer" of 1964, thousands of civil rights workers, black and white, fanned out through the South, especially in Mississippi, to register blacks as voters. Three such workers, Michael Schwerner, James Chaney, and Andrew Goodman (above), were kidnapped and killed while participating in a voter registration drive in rural Mississippi. (AP/Wide World)

▲ In the 1964 election campaign, Lyndon Johnson campaigned as a "candidate for peace," even as the nation's role in the Vietnam War was expanding. Johnson was an easy winner over Republican Barry Goldwater, whose conservative agenda divided his party.

(Lyndon Baines Johnson Library; Cecil Stoughton)

Early in August 1964, U.S. aircraft bombed North Vietnam to retaliate ▲ against "attacks" on U.S. ships. When young people held a rally in New York City's Times Square to protest the U.S. action, they were subdued by police. (AP/Wide World)

President Lyndon B. Johnson reaches to shake hands with the Reverend Martin Luther King, Jr., after signing the Voting Rights Act on August 6, 1965. The legislation authorized federal officials to register black voters in areas where discrimination existed. It also eliminated literacy tests and other devices meant to deny the vote to blacks. (AP/Wide World)

The war in Vietnam, a small country in Southeast Asia, dominated the news through much of the 1960s. From 1957 to 1965, the war was chiefly a struggle between the South Vietnamese and Communist-trained guerrillas known as Vietcong. Here, South Vietnamese army troops in combat against the Vietcong.

(National Archives)

The body of Malcolm X, black militant leader, lies in a casket in New York City. Assassinated on February 21, 1965, while giving a speech at the Audubon Ballroom in Harlem, Malcolm X, a Black Muslim minister, spoke out frequently on behalf of black separatism, nationalism, and pride. (AP/Wide World)

▼ U.S. involvement in Vietnam began expanding in 1965 and continued into 1969, when there were about 540,000 American troops in South Vietnam. But in 1969, the United States slowly began to withdraw its forces. (National Archives)

▲ When Jim Brown of the Cleveland Browns, often hailed as the best running back in professional football history, retired in 1965, he held a helmetful of rushing records, including most career touchdowns (105), most yards gained (12,312), and highest average gain per carry (5.2 yards). (CBS-TV Sports)

◀ Stokely Carmichael, head of the Student Nonviolent Coordinating Committee (SNCC) and "black power" advocate, addresses a crowd of young blacks during a demonstration in Montgomery, Alabama, in June 1967. Carmichael called for racial separatism and revolution, urging black citizens to gain control of their lives and reject white values. (AP/Wide World)

Racial tension in Watts, a depressed black section of Los Angeles, sparked a six-day riot that began on August 11, 1965. It led to thirty-four deaths, more than a thousand injuries, and four thousand arrests. Right, a California highway patrolman stands guard over a group of blacks outside a looted Watts store.

(AP/Wide World)

◀ In October 1966, President Johnson took off on a trip to Manila, in the Philippines, for a conference of leaders of seven Pacific nations. During the journey, he made a surprise visit to Cam Ranh Bay in South Vietnam, where he visited American soldiers. Later, Johnson talked about the "strong hands" he had gripped and the "quiet voices" of the wounded he visited in a hospital.

(National Archives)

◀ By 1967, U.S. involvement in Vietnam was being seriously questioned, and peace marches and protests were becoming the order of the day. Left, antiwar demonstrators, led by Coretta Scott King, wife of Martin Luther King, Jr., and author and activist Dr. Benjamin Spock, amass at the gates of the White House in May 1967.
(Lyndon B. Johnson Library; Robert Knudson)

Thurgood Marshall (right), appointed by Lyndon B. Johnson as the first ▼ black member of the U.S. Supreme Court, chats with Justice Hugo Black, who swore Marshall in on September 1, 1967. Educated at Howard University in Washington, D.C., Marshall gained national recognition as legal counsel for the NAACP (National Association for the Advancement of Colored People).

(AP/Wide World)

◀ Rejecting many of the values of their parents, hippies declared a "Summer of Love" in 1967, celebrating peace, love, and understanding. Left, hippies in San Francisco's Golden Gate Park welcome the first day of summer, June 21. As part of the celebration, they keep aloft a huge inflated ball, painted to represent the globe.
(AP/Wide World)

A U.S. gun goes into action against the North Vietnamese near Khe Sanh on January 29, 1968. For the most part, the North Vietnamese and Vietcong avoided major battles in the open, where U.S. firepower could carry the day. They preferred using guerrilla tactics, operating in small bands, tormenting Americans with quick raids and ambushes.

(AP/Wide World)

On April 4, 1968, as he leaned over the railing of a second-floor balcony at the Lorraine Motel in Memphis, Tennessee, the Reverend Martin Luther King, Jr., was shot and killed. King's murderer, James Earl Ray, was captured two months later. In this photo, taken the day before the shooting, King stands in the approximate spot on the same balcony where the shooting occurred. Standing next to King, tieless, is the Reverend Jesse Jackson; at the right is the Reverend Ralph Abernathy.

(AP/Wide World)

The mule-drawn casket of the Reverend Martin Luther King, Jr., leads thousands of marchers through the streets of Atlanta. The outpouring of grief for Dr. King was matched only by the reaction to the death of President John F. Kennedy.

(AP/Wide World)

This photograph of an execution is one of the most memorable images to come out of the Vietnam War. A Saigon police chief, Colonel Nguyen Ngoc Loan, is the man with the pistol. His target is a Vietcong guerrilla wearing civilian clothes, his hands tied behind his back, who was captured in Saigon early in 1968. Nguyen fired one shot into his prisoner's head. "They killed many Americans and many of my people," Nguyen said. (AP/Wide World)

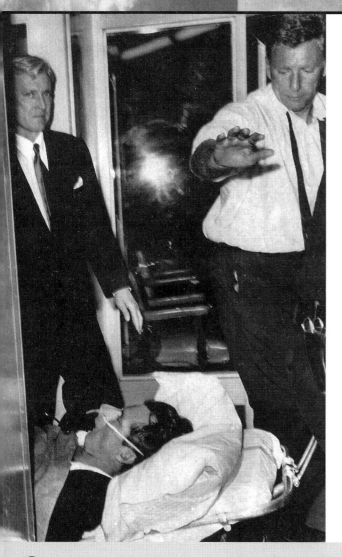

◀ Robert F. Kennedy, gravely wounded in the head, is carried into a hospital on June 6, 1968, after being shot at the Ambassador Hotel in Los Angeles. Earlier in the year, Kennedy, a brother of President John F. Kennedy, had announced his candidacy for the Democratic nomination for president. On the evening that he and his supporters learned that he had won the California primary, Kennedy was assassinated. (AP/Wide World)

▲
Shirley Chisholm gives the V for victory sign in her Brooklyn, New York, headquarters on the morning of November 6, 1968, after learning that she had been elected as the first black woman to serve in the U.S. House of Representatives. (AP/Wide World)

◄ During the Democratic Convention in Chicago in August 1968, violence and bloodshed occurred in the streets as police confronted antiwar demonstrators. In this photo, a policeman, his nightstick raised, chases a demonstrator during a clash in Chicago's Lincoln Park.
(AP/Wide World)

In the election of 1968, Republican Richard M. Nixon, promising voters law and order and "peace with honor" in Vietnam, won a narrow victory over his Democratic opponent, Vice President Hubert H. Humphrey.
(D.C. Public Library; *The Washington Star* Collection)

A powerful blast sends a *Saturn 5* rocket ▶ and its *Apollo 11* space vehicle into the air on July 16, 1969, a mission that put the first Americans — indeed, the first humans — on the surface of the moon. Four days after the launch, the landing craft carrying astronauts Neil Armstrong and Edwin E. "Buzz" Aldrin settled on the moon's surface. (NASA)

▲ An astronaut boot print on the lunar soil. In the years following the *Apollo 11* mission, other Apollo missions continued to explore the lunar surface, with astronauts collecting rock samples and installing instruments for scientific research. (NASA)

▲ Astronauts Neil Armstrong and Edwin E. "Buzz" Aldrin became the first humans to walk on the moon following the successful landing of their lunar module on the moon's surface on July 20, 1969. (NASA)

Hundreds of music fans jam the highway leaving Bethel, New York, part of the throng of more than 400,000 that gathered at a farm near Woodstock, New York, on the weekend of August 15–17, 1969, for a rock music festival. Featured were such performers and bands as The Who, Jefferson Airplane, Country Joe and the Fish, and Jimi Hendrix. (AP/Wide World)

Recycling, the process of recovering and reusing many different types of materials instead of throwing them away, took on increased importance during the late 1960s. Environmental concerns led many communities to establish curbside collection programs, with trucks picking up aluminum cans, steel cans, glass containers, and paper for reuse in the manufacturing of new products. Here, five youngsters of a Cary, North Carolina, couple climb on a huge pile of aluminum cans that they helped their father collect.
(AP/Wide World)

Silent Majority for Peace

SUPPORT

As the Vietnam War dragged on and casualty lists kept getting longer, opposition widened and deepened. Antiwar marches and protests became common. Here, a peace parade in the fall of 1969 fills Pennsylvania Avenue in Washington, D.C. (AP/Wide World)

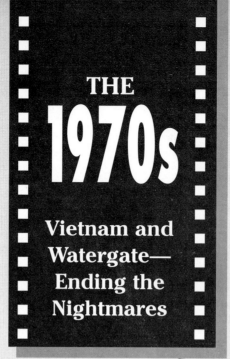

THE 1970s

Vietnam and Watergate— Ending the Nightmares

THE PEOPLE OF THE UNITED STATES had grown weary of the Vietnam War as the 1970s began. But the war dragged on. Television coverage brought images of the war's horrors into millions of American homes every night, which helped strengthen opposition to the conflict. By the 1970s, even U.S. Army troops in Vietnam were wearing love beads and peace symbols.

President Richard M. Nixon and Henry Kissinger, Nixon's chief foreign policy adviser, found a solution. On January 27, 1973, in Paris, the United States, South Vietnam, North Vietnam, and the Vietcong signed a cease-fire agreement that permitted the United States to get out of Vietnam. By March 1973, the last U.S. ground forces had left.

But the war wasn't over. With American troops gone and little in the way of support coming from the United States, the North Vietnamese and Vietcong went on the attack. On April 30, 1975, the South Vietnamese surrendered.

So ended what was the longest war in American history and the only war in which U.S. combat troops failed to achieve their goals. About fifty-eight thousand American military personnel died in the war; a third of a million were wounded. South Vietnamese losses were more than a million. Bitter and painful memories of the war endure to this day.

President Richard M. Nixon, reelected in a landslide in 1972, was not around at the war's end. He had resigned from office on August 8, 1974, following a string of political scandals known as Watergate.

On taking office, Nixon's vice president and successor, Gerald Ford, declared, "Our long national nightmare is over," referring to Watergate. Later, Ford pardoned Nixon, assuring that the former president would suffer no punishment because of the scandal.

Ford lost to Democrat Jimmy Carter in the presidential election of 1976. Carter, a former Georgia governor, stressed human rights, established a national energy policy, and brought about peace between Israel and Egypt. But in 1979, when sixty Americans from the U.S. Embassy in Tehran were taken hostage by Iranian students, Jimmy Carter was blamed. He became a one-term president.

The 1970s did have some heroes: Sam J. Ervin, Jr., senator from North Carolina, who managed the Senate's Watergate committee; Gloria Steinem, who campaigned for women's rights in employment and politics, among other things; and Ralph Nader, who stuck up for the American consumer.

Some of the popular television comedies of the 1970s had political overtones. For *All in the Family,* the subject was often race. *The Mary Tyler Moore Show* stressed gender.

There were problems in the economy in the second half of the 1970s; inflation and unemployment soared. There were also foreign policy frustrations. But the decade is remembered for Watergate and the war in Vietnam. Together they caused the American people to question their basic institutions and to look for leadership and restored confidence.

◄During the spring of 1970, Americans celebrated the first Earth Day, focusing on the nation's environmental problems. Left, a student demonstrator in New York City wears a gas mask to call attention to air pollution. (AP/Wide World)

PLEASE! PLEASE!
DO NOT SMOKE IN MEDIA
BETWEEN 11 A.M. & 12 NOON
DURING THE MONTH OF MAY
**"GIVE YOUR LUNGS A BREAK...
FOR YOUR OWN HEALTH'S SAKE"**
AMERICAN CANCER SOCIETY

The Twenty-sixth Amendment to the Constitution lowered the voting age from twenty-one to eighteen. Right, eighteen-year-olds register to vote in New York City during June 1971.►

(Library of Congress; *U.S. News & World Report* Collection)

◄When the town of Media, Pennsylvania, asked residents to stop smoking between the hours of 11 A.M. and noon during the month of May 1971, few took the campaign seriously. But what happened in Media signaled the beginning of the war against smoking and cigarettes. The same year, a ban was put on radio and TV commercials that advertised cigarettes. In 1972, manufacturers agreed to include a health warning in all cigarette advertising.

(Collection of William Welling)

In April 1970, President Richard M. Nixon ordered U.S. and South Vietnamese forces into Cambodia to destroy supply centers that the North Vietnamese had set up in that country. The invasion triggered protests on college campuses. On May 4, 1970, National Guard units fired into a group of demonstrators at Kent State University in Kent, Ohio, killing four students and wounding nine others. Photographer John Filo took this photograph of the bloody moment when a young girl bent over the body of a slain student. The photograph aroused even greater opposition to the war.

(John Filo) ►

▲

Kim Phuc was nine years old in 1972 when her family's village in Vietnam was firebombed and her body seared by napalm. This image of her is one of the most shocking and painful photographs of the Vietnam War.
(AP/Wide World)

For a generation and more, the United States and China were on unfriendly terms, each nation barely admitting that the other existed. President Nixon helped to change that by opening up a new relationship with the Chinese. Nixon startled observers in 1972 with a week-long visit to China. Below, Nixon and China's premier Zhou Enlai meet members of the media in Beijing.
(AP/Wide World) ▼

◄ In February 1973, members of the American Indian Movement (AIM) seized and occupied the town of Wounded Knee, South Dakota, site of a massacre of Sioux by federal troops in 1890. AIM sought changes in the administration of the Sioux reservation in South Dakota and demanded that the government honor treaty obligations. A clash between those occupying the town and federal forces left one Indian dead and another wounded.
(AP/Wide World)

On June 17, 1972, five men were arrested for breaking into the Democratic National Headquarters at the Watergate apartment and office complex in Washington, D.C., right. The burglars, it was found, had been hired by the Committee to Reelect the President, which supported President Nixon. The break-in led to a series of political scandals involving President Nixon that eventually brought about his resignation in 1974. (George Sullivan)

▶

With the signing of a Vietnam cease-fire agreement early in 1973, 562 American prisoners of war were released and able to return to their families. One was Lieutenant Colonel Robert L. Strim of Foster City, California. In a moment of pure joy, Strim's family rushes to greet him on his arrival at Travis Air Force Base in California.

(AP/Wide World) ▼

◄ Roberto Clemente, one of baseball's all-time greats, died in a plane crash late in 1972 while flying to aid victims of an earthquake in Nicaragua. As the right fielder for the Pittsburgh Pirates, Clemente won four National League batting titles and was named the league's Most Valuable Player in 1966. He helped lead the Pirates to World Series wins in 1960 and 1971.

(Baseball Nostalgia)

A view of Earth as photographed from the *Apollo 17* spacecraft. The last moon mission, *Apollo 17* was conducted during December 1972.

(NASA)

◄ Gloria Steinem emerged during the early 1970s as one of the nation's foremost feminist writers and political activists. In 1971, she helped to organize both the National Women's Political Caucus and the Women's Action Alliance. The following year, she was a cofounder of *Ms.* magazine, a publication that she edited until 1987.

(D.C. Library; *The Washington Star* Collection)

H. R. "Bob" Haldeman, chief of staff to President Nixon from 1969 to 1973, testifies before the Senate Watergate Committee in Washington. Haldeman was later convicted of perjury, conspiracy, and obstruction of justice in the Watergate cover-up.
(AP/Wide World) ▼

▲
Following the resignation of Vice President Spiro Agnew, Richard Nixon (left), with the approval of Congress, chose Gerald R. Ford as his vice president. Above, Ford and Nixon pose at the White House after Ford's confirmation as vice president.

(From the collection of Alex Tabourin)

In 1973, members of OPEC, the Organization of Petroleum Exporting Countries, announced a ban on petroleum shipments to nations that supported Israel. At the same time, OPEC raised petroleum prices by four hundred percent. The resulting fuel shortage caused chaos at gas stations, as motorists lined up for fuel.
(AP/Wide World)

The Nixon administration's cover-up and obstruction of justice following the Watergate break-in eventually led to a recommendation by a congressional committee that Nixon be impeached, that is, charged with misconduct in office. To avoid impeachment, Nixon resigned, the first president of the United States to do so. In this photograph, taken on August 9, 1974, Nixon and his wife, Pat, stand together following Nixon's farewell remarks to his White House staff. (AP/Wide World) ▼

Hank Aaron, home-run hero of the Atlanta Braves, watches the flight of the ball after hitting his 715th homer on April 8, 1974, in a game against the Los Angeles Dodgers. The blast enabled Aaron to top Babe Ruth's 714 career home runs, a record that had endured for thirty-nine years. Aaron was elected to baseball's Hall of Fame in 1982. (AP/Wide World)

▲ With Nixon's resignation, Gerald Ford became president. Above, Ford, with his wife, Betty, looking on, takes the oath of office on August 9, 1974. (AP/Wide World)

▲ *Star Wars*, a science-fiction movie, was released in 1977. No one was prepared for its enormous success. *Star Wars* won seven Oscars, shattered all box-office records, and led to the production of two sequels. (Movie Star News)

Jimmy and Rosalynn Carter surprised crowds on Carter's inauguration day, January 20, 1977, by forsaking the presidential limousine to walk down Pennsylvania Avenue from the Capitol to the White House. Not since Thomas Jefferson had a president of the United States walked in his inauguration parade. (AP/Wide World) ▼

Lynette "Squeaky" Fromme was taken into custody by federal authorities after attempting to assassinate President Ford outside the state capitol in Sacramento, California. "The country is a mess!" Fromme shouted at the sight of Ford. "This man is not your president." (AP/Wide World) ▼

During his twenty-nine months in office, President Ford survived two assassination attempts. Both occurred in September 1975. Ford is pictured below during the first attempt, in a park in Sacramento, California. The second attack took place outside the St. Francis Hotel in San Francisco. In each case, the would-be assassin was captured, tried, and given a lifetime prison sentence. (AP/Wide World) ▼

President Jimmy Carter (center) served as a historic peacemaker between Egypt and Israel by holding talks at the president's Camp David retreat with Egypt's president Anwar Sadat (left) and Israel's prime minister Menachem Begin. After long negotiations, a formal peace treaty between the two countries, known as the Camp David Accords, was signed.

(AP/Wide World)

A nuclear reactor at the Three Mile Island power plant near Harrisburg, Pennsylvania, suffered a partial core meltdown on March 28, 1979, resulting in the release of radioactive gases into the atmosphere. About 100,000 residents of the area had to be evacuated.

(AP/Wide World)

An armed mob of Iranians invaded the American Embassy in Iran on November 4, 1979, seized military and diplomatic personnel inside, and held them as hostages. In this photo taken from a television monitor, a blindfolded hostage is paraded about outside the embassy. The mob demanded the return of the Shah of Iran, who was in the United States at the time, in exchange for the hostages' freedom. Fifty-three Americans were kept prisoners in the embassy for more than a year.

(AP/Wide World)

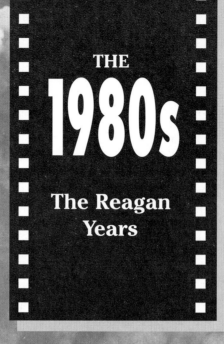

THE 1980s

The Reagan Years

RONALD REAGAN WAS ELECTED president of the United States in 1980 and became the decade's dominant political figure. He proposed changes in government more startling than any since Franklin Roosevelt's New Deal more than fifty years before. The former movie actor and California governor set out to cut taxes, reduce government regulations, and shrink the federal deficit. At the same time, he sought to combat the Soviet Union and nations friendly to it — the Evil Empire, Reagan called it — in every corner of the globe.

Grappling with the Soviet Union and its supporters was expensive, requiring a lavish military buildup. By 1989, the federal government was spending $303 billion a year on defense, or more than $500,000 a minute.

The enormous popularity that Reagan enjoyed, which led to his reelection in 1984 by an overwhelming majority, was not based on his political agenda alone. Reagan had the ability to express a view of America that stressed "old-fashioned" values — patriotism, hard work, self-reliance, and family togetherness. People liked that. The Great Communicator, he was called.

The nation faced several serious problems during the 1980s. Crime rates swelled, chiefly because of a jump in drug-related offenses. Crack, derived from cocaine, was often the drug of choice. A growing number of homeless men and women camped out on the streets of American cities. Critics noted that the administration offered no solution to such problems.

The government was also criticized for not doing enough after AIDS (Acquired Immune Deficiency Syndrome), a deadly new disease, surfaced. Caused by a virus that destroys the body's immune system, AIDS reached near-epidemic proportions during the 1980s.

The darkest cloud over the White House during the Reagan years resulted from the administration's willingness to occasionally advance its foreign policy goals by secret means. The most glaring example was Reagan's itch to support the Contras, a group of Nicaraguan rebels intent on taking over the government of Nicaragua. This resulted in what came to be known as the Iran-Contra scandal.

Such missteps, however, scarcely affected Reagan's personal appeal. He was as popular on the day he left office as on the day he entered it.

George Bush, who served as vice president during Ronald Reagan's eight years in office, won the presidential election of 1988, thanks, at least in part, to his strong ties to Reagan.

But for Bush it was different. He lacked Reagan's appeal. When he sought reelection in 1992, he lost to the individual who would become the dominant political figure of the 1990s, former Arkansas governor Bill Clinton.

At 8:32 A.M. on Sunday, May 18, 1980, Mount Saint Helens, a snow-capped 8,364-foot peak in Vancouver in southwest Washington State, blew its top. The eruption sent a plume of smoke and ash thirteen miles into the air, dusting cities and farms in four states.

(AP/Wide World)

John Lennon, a former member of the Beatles, was shot to death outside his New York City apartment on December 8, 1980. Twenty-five-year-old Mark David Chapman was his assassin. Right, Lennon performs at a concert at New York City's Madison Square Garden in 1972.

(AP/Wide World)

On January 20, 1981, the day of Ronald Reagan's inauguration, the American hostages in Iran boarded a plane to freedom after an ordeal that had lasted 444 days. Left, three of the former hostages, heading for the United States, wave to a welcoming crowd.

(AP/Wide World)

Ronald Reagan swept to victory over Jimmy Carter in the presidential election of 1980. Reagan, who enjoyed relaxing at his ranch in the mountains near Santa Barbara, California, was one of the most popular presidents of the twentieth century.

(Ronald Reagan Library)

Released in 1982, *ET: The Extra Terrestrial* became the biggest box-office hit in motion picture history up to that time. Moviegoers of all ages were charmed by the film.
(Movie Star News)

▲ Appointed by President Ronald Reagan in 1981, Sandra Day O'Connor was the first female justice of the Supreme Court. A lawyer and former majority leader of the Arizona State Senate, Justice O'Connor served in the Arizona Superior Court before her appointment to the Supreme Court. She is pictured, above, after delivering the commencement address at Wheaton College in Norton, Massachusetts, in 1985.
(AP/Wide World)

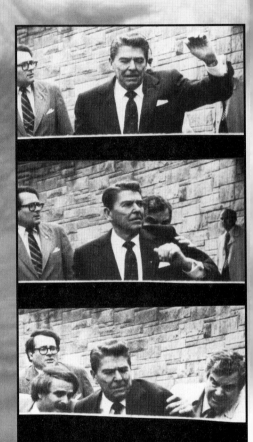

Only seventy days after his inauguration, Ronald Reagan was the victim of an assassination attempt outside a Washington, D.C., hotel where he had just delivered a speech. Wounded in the chest, the president was rushed to a nearby hospital where doctors repaired the damage. Reagan made a speedy recovery. (AP/Wide World)

John Hinckley, Jr., a twenty-five-year-old drifter from Evergreen, Colorado, shot Reagan and three others in the assassination attempt. A jury found Hinckley to be insane, and he was placed in a mental institution. (AP/Wide World) ▶

Not long after 6 A.M. on Sunday, October 23, 1983, a suicide truck loaded with explosives rammed its way into the lobby of a barrack at the Beirut (Lebanon) International Airport, where marines of a U.S. peace-keeping force were quartered. When the deadly cargo exploded, the building collapsed and 240 marines died. Here, rescue workers carry the body of a marine killed in the blast.
(AP/Wide World)

Chosen by Democratic presidential candidate Walter Mondale as his running mate in 1984, Geraldine Ferraro was the first woman vice presidential candidate of a major party. Above, a jubilant Ferraro is pictured at the Democratic National Convention in San Francisco; Mondale stands just behind her.
(AP/Wide World)

◄ In June 1983, Sally Ride became the first American woman to travel in space when she made a six-day flight aboard the space shuttle *Challenger*. Ride took part in a second space flight in October 1984.
(NASA)

Tragedy struck the space program of the United States on January 28, 1986, when the space shuttle *Challenger* exploded in a ball of fire shortly after takeoff from the Kennedy Space Center in Florida, bringing death to the *Challenger*'s crew of seven. It was the worst accident in the history of the space program.

(AP/Wide World)

In 1986, Congress established January 15, the birth date of slain civil rights leader Martin Luther King, Jr., as a national holiday to be celebrated on the third Monday in January. In this photograph, LaRose Housworth attends a candlelight vigil at King's tomb.

(AP/Wide World) ▲

Marine Lieutenant Colonel Oliver North became the central figure in a secret and illegal effort by officials of the Reagan administration to sell U.S. weapons to Iran during 1986, with the profits going to American-backed rebels — the Contras — in Nicaragua.

(AP/Wide World)

◀ Ronald Reagan (right) and George Bush won another landslide election victory in 1984, defeating the Democratic ticket of Walter Mondale and Geraldine Ferraro.

(The White House; Michael Evans)

▲

The Reverend Jesse Jackson gives the thumbs-up sign to youngsters at the Head Start Childcare Center in Sacramento, California, during his campaign for the Democratic nomination for president in the spring of 1988. Though he failed in his quest, Jackson is recognized as the first black person to emerge as a serious contender for the presidency. (AP/Wide World)

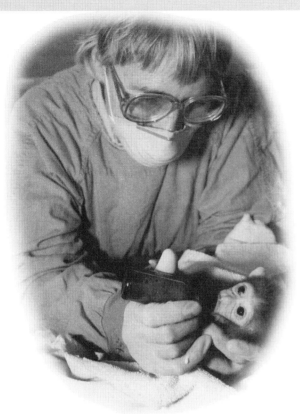

▲

U.S. officials announced in 1986 that cases of AIDS (Acquired Immune Deficiency Syndrome) would increase tenfold by the end of the decade. Above, a three-week-old macaque monkey is fed by a laboratory technician. Macaques were found to be valuable to scientists studying AIDS after it was discovered that the animals were dying of the disease. (AP/Wide World)

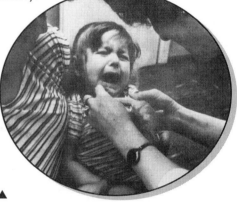

▲

The worst accident in the history of nuclear energy took place at the nuclear power plant Chernobyl in the Soviet Union in April 1986 when the cooling system in a nuclear reactor failed. The reactor's core then overheated and melted down. The fire and explosion that followed brought death and suffering to thousands in the area and sent up a vapor cloud of radioactivity that drifted over much of the planet. Above, a nurse at a children's health clinic in Warsaw, Poland, administers an iodine solution to a three-year-old girl as a protection from radiation poisoning. (AP/Wide World)

◀ After President Ronald Reagan (right) and Soviet leader Mikhail Gorbachev had exchanged visits, the two nations entered into a treaty that eliminated American and Soviet intermediate-range nuclear missiles from Europe. Left, Gorbachev arrives at the White House. (AP/Wide World)

On March 24, 1989, the oil tanker *Exxon Valdez*, bound from Valdez, Alaska, slammed into an undersea reef, releasing nearly eleven million gallons of crude oil into the waters of Alaska's Prince William Sound, one of the most environmentally sensitive areas in North America. The biggest oil spill in U.S. history, it devastated wildlife, killing thousands of sea otters, bald eagles, sea ducks, loons, cormorants, and other species. Here, in a photo taken some two weeks after the disaster, the *Exxon Valdez* awaits repairs while anchored in Prince William Sound. (AP/Wide World)

Thanks to his devastating dunks, fancy finger rolls, and unstoppable skyhooks, Kareem Abdul-Jabbar ranked as the greatest point scorer in pro basketball history when he retired in 1989 after twenty seasons of competition. The twenty-three records he held included most points (38,387), most field goals (15,837), and most games played (1,560). ▶
(George Sullivan)

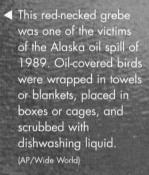

◀ This red-necked grebe was one of the victims of the Alaska oil spill of 1989. Oil-covered birds were wrapped in towels or blankets, placed in boxes or cages, and scrubbed with dishwashing liquid. (AP/Wide World)

The Soviet Union broke up and the Communist parties of Eastern ▶ Europe collapsed in 1989, mind-boggling events that were symbolized by the dismantling of the Berlin Wall. Located between East and West Berlin in East Germany, the wall had stood as a symbol of the Cold War for nearly thirty years. (AP/Wide World)

The popularity of Rap, a form of music that is spoken to a beat, mushroomed in popularity in the 1980s. The most popular rappers included M. C. Hammer (above), Ice-T, Run-DMC, Dr. Dre, and the Beastie Boys.
(AP/Wide World)

Late in 1989, President George Bush sent American troops into Panama to overthrow Panamanian military leader Manuel Noriega, believed to be a major drug trafficker. Below, an American soldier armed with a heavy caliber automatic weapon searches for a sniper in Panama City. Noriega was captured, brought to the United States, tried, found guilty, and sent to prison.
(AP/Wide World) ▼

A major earthquake struck the San Jose–San Francisco–Oakland area of California on October 17, 1989, causing sixty-two deaths and millions of dollars in property damage. Twelve of the deaths resulted when the top section of an interstate freeway collapsed in Oakland onto its lower level, crushing dozens of vehicles.
(AP/Wide World)

THE 1990s

The Coming Millennium

As THE 1990s BEGAN, THE United States — indeed, the free world — could rejoice in the fact that the Communist governments of the Soviet Union and Eastern Europe had self-destructed. The Cold War was now history. The more than forty years of hostility between the United States and the Soviet Union that made nuclear war an almost constant threat was over. "We have slain a very large dragon," James Woolsey, director of the Central Intelligence Agency, said to Congress.

With the absence of the Cold War, foreign policy specialists had to rethink the role of the United States, the only remaining superpower. What do we do now was the question that faced George Bush, who held the presidency at the beginning of the decade, and Bill Clinton, who succeeded Bush in 1993.

Despite the Cold War's end, the world was not without its dangers. The collapse of Communism led to the release of ethnic fears and hatreds, tearing nations apart. The Sudan, India, and the former Yugoslavia were only three examples.

The United States had ethnic concerns of its own. Through most of the nation's history, U.S. citizens thought of themselves pretty much as a society of two races: whites and blacks. By the beginning of the 1990s, that was no longer true.

The number of immigrants arriving from Latin America, the Caribbean, and Asia, once a trickle, grew rapidly during the 1970s and 1980s. As a result, Hispanics and Asians had become important segments of the nation's population.

With the nation enjoying peace as well as prosperous times and low unemployment, the media's focus turned to celebrities. The so-called Trial of the Century, in which O. J. Simpson was tried for the murder of his ex-wife and a male friend of hers, got lavish daily television and newspaper coverage for nine months. The tragic death of Diana, Princess of Wales, in a car crash in Paris in 1997 also led to overwhelming media attention.

Bill Clinton was reelected in 1996, easily turning aside a challenge from Republican Bob Dole, the former Senate majority leader. As the year 2000 drew near, President Clinton was cheered by the fact that the American economy hummed along at a lively pace — thanks to low inflation, low unemployment, and strong corporate profits.

But it was not a golden time. It wasn't like the 1950s or 1960s, when most families had one earner. Now two or more people worked in most households. And the typical earner often worked longer hours as well.

It was still possible to enjoy the good times and the fruits of the American dream. But doing so meant working harder.

In February 1991, as the Iraqi army retreated following an attack by U.S.-led forces, Iraqi troops sabotaged hundreds of oil wells, leaving a black pall of smoke over much of Kuwait. Here, flames and thick smoke billow up from an oil well in Kuwait. (AP/Wide World)

Madonna and ▶
Michael Jackson
continued their
reigns as pop
superstars through
the first half of the
1990s. Right, the two
arrive at a Los Angeles
restaurant for dinner early
in April 1991. (AP/Wide World)

▼ The Persian Gulf War, a conflict between an alliance of forces led by
the United States and the Iraqi army under Saddam Hussein, erupted
on August 2, 1990, after Iraq invaded Kuwait, Iraq's tiny neighbor to
the south, and threatened to take control of oil supplies in the region.
In Operation Desert Storm, Allied planes began an air assault on Iraq
and Kuwait in an effort to force the Iraqi army out of Kuwait.

(U.S. Air Force; SSgt F. Lee Corkran)

▲
A weapons maintenance specialist loads a Sidewinder
air-to-air missile onto an F-16 fighter at a U.S. air base
on the southern Arabian Peninsula in February 1991
during the Persian Gulf War. (AP/Wide World)

◀ Homeless people outside the Fred Jordan Mission in Los Angeles wait for lunch. A tightening recession forced more than two million Americans into poverty during 1991, bringing the number of people officially classified as poor to its highest point in twenty-seven years.

(AP/Wide World)

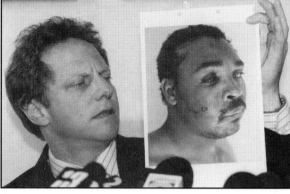

▲

In April 1992, a jury that included no blacks acquitted four policemen on all but one count in the beating of Rodney King, a black man. Soon after the verdict, a wave of rioting, looting, and violence swept south-central Los Angeles. Fifty-two people died and more than six hundred buildings were set aflame. Above, King's lawyer displays a photo of his client during a press conference at his office in Los Angeles.

(AP/Wide World)

A powerful hurricane named Andrew, ▶ one of the worst natural disasters ever to strike the United States, devastated south Florida on August 24, 1992, taking fourteen lives, destroying or damaging 85,000 homes, and leaving some 250,000 people homeless. Right, food is distributed to survivors in South Dade County several days after the hurricane.

(AP/Wide World)

Democratic candidate Bill Clinton ▶ leads a throng of joggers down Pennsylvania Avenue in Washington, D.C., during his first campaign for the presidency in 1992. In the election in November, Clinton and vice presidential candidate Al Gore won by a comfortable margin over President George Bush and Independent candidate H. Ross Perot. (AP/Wide World)

In December 1992, the United Nations accepted an offer by the United States to safeguard the delivery of food supplies to the starving people of Somalia. Here, U.S. Marines from Camp Pendleton, California, arrive at the main airport in Mogadishu. (AP/Wide World)

◄ Winner of the demanding heptathlon, a track and field contest combining seven different events, in both the 1988 and 1992 Olympic Games, Jackie Joyner-Kersee of the United States also won billing as the world's greatest female athlete. During her career, Joyner-Kersee won a total of six Olympic medals and set five world records. (AP/Wide World)

▲ President Clinton appointed Janet Reno to be attorney general in his cabinet in 1993. The chief state prosecutor in Miami, Florida, Reno was the first woman to hold the attorney general's post. (AP/Wide World)

◄ A powerful bomb exploded in an underground parking garage of the World Trade Center in New York City on February 26, 1993, killing six people and injuring more than a thousand others. Islamic extremists were found guilty of the bombing and sentenced to long prison terms. Left, a victim is aided by a New York City police officer. (AP/Wide World)

Nine midwestern states were battered by the great flood of 1993, which took more than fifty lives, left some 70,000 homeless, and caused approximately $12 billion in property damage. Right, a man rows his way down a flooded street in Davenport, Iowa. (AP/Wide World)

ROAD CLOSED

▲
A predawn earthquake struck Los Angeles on January 17, 1994, taking sixty-one lives and causing widespread destruction. About forty-five thousand homes and apartments were damaged or destroyed. Above, an unidentified store worker walks amid merchandise strewn about the floor of a Los Angeles grocery store. (AP/Wide World)

◀ President Clinton presides over a handshake of peace on the White House lawn between Yitzhak Rabin, Israel's prime minister (left), and Yasir Arafat, chairman of the Palestine Liberation Organization. The ceremonies marked the signing of the 1993 peace accord between Israel and the Palestinians.
(AP/Wide World)

Called boat people, Cubans desperate to come to the ▶
United States to escape poverty and hunger flooded
into the United States during the early 1990s,
heading north toward Florida in tiny boats,
on rafts, and even on wooden planks. A
revised emigration agreement between
the United States and Cuba in September
1994 sharply reduced the flight of boat
people after more than thirty thousand
had left Cuba. (AP/Wide World)

◀ Major league baseball
players went on strike
on August 11, 1994.
On the thirty-fourth
day of the strike, the
team owners canceled
the rest of the season.
For the first time since
1904, there was no
World Series and no
world champion team.
(AP/Wide World)

U.S. forces were poised to invade the ▶
troubled island of Haiti in the West
Indies in September 1994. But at the
last minute, Haiti's military leaders
agreed to step down and turn the
government over to President Jean-
Bertrand Aristide. Eventually, however,
twenty-one thousand U.S. troops landed
on the island in a peace-keeping
operation. (AP/Wide World)

◀ In what was called the Trial of the Century, sportscaster, actor, and former football superstar O. J. Simpson was tried for the murders of his ex-wife Nicole Brown Simpson and her friend Ron Goldman. On October 3, 1995, after a 266-day trial followed daily on television by millions, the jury, deliberating for only four hours, found Simpson not guilty. Left, Simpson as the verdict was being read. Holding Simpson is attorney Johnnie Cochran. Others include, from left, F. Lee Bailey and Robert Kardashian. In 1997, a civil jury found Simpson liable for the deaths of his ex-wife and Ron Goldman. (AP/Wide World)

The north side of the Alfred P. Murrah Federal Building in Oklahoma City, Oklahoma, is missing after a bomb left in a truck exploded outside the building on April 19, 1995. The explosion caused the death of 169 people, including nineteen young children and one rescue worker. More than four hundred people were injured. Timothy McVeigh was found guilty of the bombing and sentenced to death. (AP/Wide World)

The warring parties in Bosnia and Herzegovina reached an agreement in November 1995 to end their conflict. Some twenty thousand U.S. troops were then sent to the troubled country to enforce the peace agreement, part of a NATO (North Atlantic Treaty Organization) security force of sixty thousand. Below, U.S. Marines arrive at the airport in Sarajevo, Bosnia. (AP/Wide World)

▼

◄ Diana, Princess of Wales, died in a car crash in Paris on August 31, 1997. Dodi Fayed, a frequent companion of Diana, was also killed in the accident. Diana's death triggered a worldwide outpouring of grief and affection. Left, a mourner attends a memorial service in honor of the princess in New York City's Central Park on September 14, 1997. (AP/Wide World)

Hundreds of thousands of men, most of them black, gathered in Washington, D.C., on October 16, 1995, to participate in the Million Man March. The "holy day of atonement and reconciliation" was inspired and organized by Louis Farrakhan, leader of the Nation of Islam. (AP/Wide World)

Mark McGwire of the St. Louis Cardinals climaxed the 1998 baseball season by breaking one of the sport's most hallowed records, Roger Maris's single season mark of 61 home runs, set in 1961. (AP/Wide World) ▼

In the great homer race of 1998, Sammy Sosa of the Chicago Cubs followed Mark McGwire in topping Roger Maris's major league record. (AP/Wide World)

Released in late 1997, *Titanic* came to rank as the most successful ▶ movie ever, the first to rake in more than $1 billion at the box office. The film stars Leonardo DiCaprio and Kate Winslet as lovers aboard the doomed ship. (Movie Star News)